thoughts

Tionne "T-Boz" Watkins

thoughts

Tionne "T-Boz"

HarperEntertainment
An Imprint of HarperCollins*Publishers*

Watkins

I dedicate *Thoughts* to my GRANDMOTHER VELMA,
who was always proud of all my accomplishments. I chose
November 3rd as the day to release *Thoughts* because it's the
first anniversary of her passing. I know she would want me to
keep living a joyful life, and now November 3rd will no longer
be an unhappy memory, but in my mind, a day to smile again.

THOUGHTS.
Copyright ©1999 by Tionne "T-Boz" Watkins for SHEE
Entertainment. All rights reserved. Printed in the United States of
America. No part of this book may be used or reproduced in any
manner whatsoever without written permission except in the case
of brief quotations embodied in critical articles and reviews. For
information address HarperCollins Publishers
Inc., 10 East 53rd Street, New York, NY 10022–5299.

HarperCollins books may be purchased for educational, business,
or sales promotional use. For information please write: Special
Markets Department, HarperCollins Publishers Inc., 10 East 53rd
Street, New York, NY 10022–5299.

FIRST EDITION

Creative Direction: Tionne "T-Boz" Watkins
Poem Artwork Photography: Ben Brown
Book Design: Lauren Holley of Howington Black
Jeannette Jacobs and Susan Sanguily of HarperCollins

Library of Congress Cataloging-in-Publication Data is available.

ISBN 0-06-105183-7

99 00 01 02 03   10 9 8 7 6 5 4 3 2 1

Tionne's Thank Yous

You have always made it possible for me to make a way out of no way. You have blessed me at times when even I questioned my worth. The times I've walked to the left, you steered me right. You know my heart and I thank you for blessing me with yours. Thank you, Lord, for watching over me.

Mom, you know how I feel. I am you and you are me. Best friends and soul mates for life.
Koko, you are my heart—I love you.
Thank you to all my friends for your love and support.
Thank you to my family for all the love and memories.

Michael Alford, thanks for helping to coordinate my book.
Nechole Murchison, my assistant, thanks for letting me get on your nerves.
Dolly Turner, my manager, thanks for all your hard work.

Ben, you were there in the beginning stages of my book. Thank you for your creative eye and for helping to bring my dream to a reality.
Lauren, thank you for your creativity.

My wonderful publisher, HarperCollins:
Mauro, thank you for your hard work, words of wisdom, and patience.
John Silbersack, thanks for believing.
Jane Friedman, Cathy Hemming, Toisan Craigg, Anja Schmidt, Amy Wasserman, Wendy Langer, Laura Leonard, Susan Sanguily, Jeannette Jacobs, Dianne Walber, Chris McKerrow, Danielle Cumbo, Michael Morrison, Brenda Segal, Steven Sorrentino, David Wolfson, Rick Harris, Josh Behar, Tavia Kowalchek, Ann Gaudinier—thanks for all your hard work and support, I appreciate you all.

Publicists: Chrisette Suter, Dvora Vener, Troy Nankin, Lorraine Sanabria.
Photographers: Ben Brown, Jon Ragel, Tom and Donnelle Smugala, Dah-Len, Marc Baptiste, Seb Janiak.
Attorneys: Fred Goldring, Seth Lichtenstein, Johnathan Haft.
Studios: Monica (Darp) Doppler, Patchwerks, Enterprise, Sterling.
Staffs of: LaFace, Arista, BMG, MP3 Com, Fan Asylum.
Make-up Artists: Yolanda Frederick, Paul Starr, Kevyn Aucoin, Jay Manuelle, Troy.
Hairstylists: Marie Davis, Machell Johnson, Carla Harrison, Gail Hudson-Ashe, Billy B. My one and only stylist: Julie Mijares.

Thanks to my wonderful fans.
Thanks so much to everyone who gave me quotes. I appreciate you all for being so thoughtful. Thanks to everyone I've ever worked with, touched, talked to, or shared kisses with, to add to my memories.

And last but not least, thanks to my "96 Roses," I have a reason to be happy again. Thanks for the beginning of something very special.

contents

preface viii

p o e m s
intro
> *i've thought* *3*

feelings
> *unpretty* *5*
> *bitter* *7*
> *the mirror* *9*
> *hatred* *11*
> *confused* *13*
> *that's a child* *15*
> *a killer* *17*

relax
> *take a deep breath* *19*
> *special* *21*
> *cherish* *23*
> *it's just a problem* *25*

e s s a y s
> *ten fan questions* *33*
> *grandma velma* *34*
> *from des moines to the dirty south* *43*
> *koko* *47*
> *high school* *50*
> *get a j-o-b* *54*
> *gayle* *58*

p o e m s
> *the voice* *63*
> *weight* *65*
> *parenthood* *67*
> *racism* *69*
> *tears* *71*

you *73*

celebrities *75*

get a j-o-b *77*

crime *78*

groupism *79*

e s s a y s

TLC *80*

jellybeans *88*

there's no business... . . . .*90*

waiting for daddy *96*

unpretty *101*

monster in my veins *106*

the thoughts behind my poems *111*

daily top 20 list *118*

aww, you shouldn't have 120

fan list 123

p o e m s
self

i wanna be free *135*

a sick life *137*

life

what's my name *139*

why *141*

wishes *143*

it's murder *145*

for sale *147*

not a punk *149*

priorities *151*

late night calls *153*

the groupie *155*

outro

mother *157*

my favorite things *159*

One night, I was sitting alone in my hotel room at the Mondrian in L.A. My then-boyfriend had just left me to go out with his friends, and I was upset. I was already feeling down because I was ill and this just made me feel that much worse. I looked okay on the outside, but on the inside I felt weak. I just couldn't

Preface

express myself to my boyfriend to let him know I wanted him to stay with me. I don't think he would have stayed anyway, which hurt, too.

I switched on the TV. Flipping through the channels, I found a talk show about men who abuse their over-weight wives. The women were filled with so much pain and unhappiness. I felt bad that night, but not like these tortured women. When the show was over, I switched off the TV and thought about all the women in the world who feel they are too skinny or too fat, too tall or too short, those who don't feel attractive. We all have something in common. At times, we've all felt unpretty, not good enough, lonely, unloved. Why did we feel this way and how does it start? Most of the time it's other people causing these bad feelings to surface. Relation-ships can be a beautiful thing, but they have an ugly side, too. I bet you that between us we know lots of people who have relationship problems, not only with the opposite sex, but also with their brothers and sisters, mothers and fathers. So I wrote "Unpretty" for all of us. That was the first poem I had ever written. Then I wrote the poem "Weight." Next thing you know, I looked up and I had written five poems. They all just flowed right out. I called my friend Salita, who is also a writer, and I read her my work. She gave me her words of wisdom and expertise, which inspired me as well.

With that I wondered, why not write a book of thoughts? Why not write about things I think about and situations I have seen or heard of? I've never been into poetry, but these pieces were from the heart and they were my art. I'm the type of person who thinks a lot. I observe people and my surround-ings closely. I listen when people speak and I often read between the lines. All these observations and impressions build up inside me, and ultimately they're expressed through my music. Usually. But TLC was between albums, and I had no other way to release myself. Finally, I had found a viable alter-native to my music.

Whether my words or experiences cause a reader to see herself, or to think about certain situations in life that need to come to the surface, or even just to make her relax and clear the air, I hope sharing *Thoughts* will make a posi-tive impact. I know writing this book has been therapeutic for me. Who knows—it might be therapeutic for others, too. It has certainly helped me to come to terms with important issues in my life and move on.

I also hope that people will have a better understanding of who I am as a person, and not just as a member of TLC. I can only express myself so much through our songs. On my own, though, I can let people into my heart and mind.

Thank you for allowing me to share my *Thoughts*.

i've watched
grown
made mistakes
listened
experienced
reached
won
loved
disliked
gave
helped
learned
lost
survived

i've thought

i've thought of all i've been through
yet i stand here still to live
god has blessed me
and to him my heart i give!
to allow me to get through
all i've done
to love me unconditionally
as he does everyone
i know i am here for a reason
that's why his grace has covered me so
i hope i get better and better
and believe me
i've thought about it, you know?

if i were you
i wish we could change shoes
because i would make you feel
unpretty too

i was told i was beautiful
but what does that mean
when you're never secure in relationships
because your man is always in between

my outsides look happy
but my insides are blue
feeling so ugly about myself
and it's all because of you

other women can't offer
what i have to give
while you're out having fun
my heart feels like it can't live

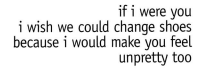

when you need someone to be around
i'm always there
but at those times
what happened to
which one was it?
the one with the long hair?

games people play and i still stay the same
but at the end of the day
i have myself to blame

it was i who was pretty
and you who was not
being with those other ones
just makes me available
and more hot

back out on the market
this is true indeed
while you're with no one
it is i who did succeed

and i am pretty!

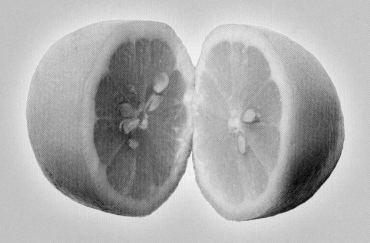

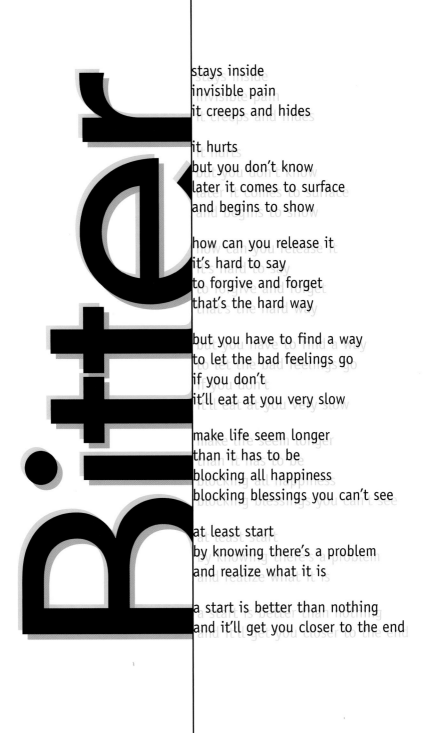

Bitter

stays inside
invisible pain
it creeps and hides

it hurts
but you don't know
later it comes to surface
and begins to show

how can you release it
it's hard to say
to forgive and forget
that's the hard way

but you have to find a way
to let the bad feelings go
if you don't
it'll eat at you very slow

make life seem longer
than it has to be
blocking all happiness
blocking blessings you can't see

at least start
by knowing there's a problem
and realize what it is

a start is better than nothing
and it'll get you closer to the end

the mirror

one day i
took a look in the mirror
and what did i see
i didn't see myself looking
back at me

who am i
i'm not the person
i used to know
i wondered why and
where did my person go

have i taken things
for granted
and let things get
beneath me
things of no substance
and that shouldn't mean
a thing to me

life changes like weather
you have ups and downs
but mostly petty things
brought about my frowns

i overlooked the real
joy of life and what
it should mean
there's so many ones
unfortunate not to see
what we've seen

i made a promise to myself
to keep my joy
and to stop giving it to someone else

not to let negative people
change me or my heart
looking in the mirror
is how i get my start

misery loves company
why should i be unhappy
because of you

i've looked myself in the mirror
and so should you

HATRED

hate is evil
hate is not good
hate makes you do things
you never thought you would

hate gets you nowhere
hate steals joy
hate is deep within
the lost hearts of girls and boys

it holds you back
makes life pass you by
makes you wonder why

why did i do this?
how could i let this be?
allowing evil to control me

dig deep within
understand yourself
know how feelings surface
the root of inner self

work against hatred
it's not your friend
unnecessary baggage
tie the loose ends

release evil feelings
replace them with love
let your heart stay pure
no hate says the man above

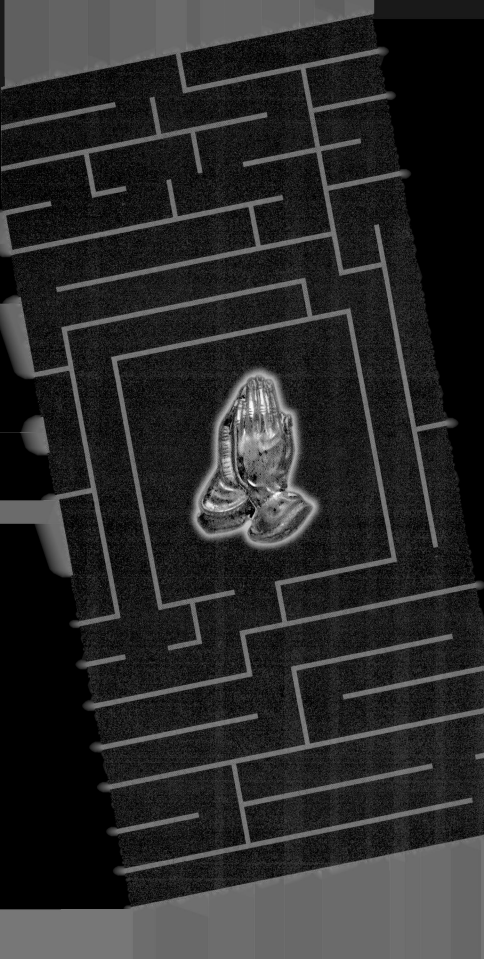

confused

don't judge
don't feel different
if you're ashamed
of what you do
then maybe there's
something wrong with it

be who you are
and feel good about yourself
if you're a freak,
speak
if you're gay,
say okay
if you're proud,
stay wild

but if you're wrong
your life will be real long

13

that's A child

how can you abuse a child
what's wrong with you
it makes it even worse
if it's ever happened to you

the world starts with our parents
don't you see
how we grow up in life
we carry for eternity

how can a child
ever have a chance
when all they see
is that adult pulling down his pants

think about what you're doing
what goes through your brain
molesting children is sick
seek help, you're insane

if it happens to you
know it's not your fault
tell someone and get help
make sure that person is caught

a killer

when you mess with me
you don't know what you've done
because i say nothing
you think you've won

i constantly think why
and the pain runs deep
the thoughts stay in my mind
and i see them in my sleep

some are born in this world
bad seed from the start
feeling good giving pain
having no soul or heart

you've made me feel things
that i don't like to feel

now thank yourself for me
because you taught me
how to kill

17

breath
take a deep

taking a deep breath
comes from deep inside
release some problems
relax, prepare for a ride

it lets off pressure
and eases tension
let go of a little stress
bitterness causes illness
i thought i should mention

calm down and breathe
let your body go
ignore chaos around you
remember breathe s-l-o-w

soothe your nerves
it does help
by taking deep breaths
you're only helping yourself

release it

s p e

cial

feeling special
is hard to do
when the world is so crazy
and seems it's all on you

feeling special
some people will never feel
so many things have
happened to some
their hearts will never heal

if you have anything in life
to feel special about
keep it with you forever
and never let it out

anything counts
if it made you feel good
feel special, feel special
unhealed hearts
wish they could

21

cherish

humans can be the worst animals
some real sweet or just plain evil
ones who are giving and caring
some who are downright deceitful

dogs are man's best friend
some lick for kisses or bite because
sometimes pets are the only animals
we learn to love
we long for unconditional love
if you can't trust humans
who can you trust?
pets always seem to believe in us

animals are precious
nature is too
we should cherish natural things
more than we do

the world is on your shoulders
so how will you cope
by taking another drink
or simply doing some dope

a child starves in africa
in his eyes the world is never seen
never knowing life for what it is
not even knowing how to dream

people die everyday
going through so much pain
yet have a positive attitude
but over the smallest thing we complain

count your blessings
god gave you a choice
if you choose the wrong things
maybe you listened to the wrong voice

don't let just a problem
bring your whole life down
someone's always worse off
think of that and remove that frown

you can overcome anything
just have faith and believe
if you failed that was your choice
and you let the devil succeed

it's just a problem

1 Tae, me, and Yolonda in '93.   2 Hot 97.5 Radio, Atlanta—Ryan
Cameron and me, in '94.   3 Face, Jon B, and TLC in the studio in '94, for
crazysexycool.   4 Cousin Tiasan in '95.   5 Salita and me.   6 In the L.A.
hotel, before the '95 AMA Awards.   7 Devyne and me.   8 Garfield and me.

1 On my 28th birthday, Jermaine Dupri gave me a '70s surprise party! Here I'm cutting my cake.   2 Darryl, Sterling, JD, Eddie, and Richard. 3 Rico Wade and me.   4 At my 29th birthday party, on April 29, 1999, held at the Imperial Fez, I'm opening my gift from my lil' brother. Happy happy joy joy. I love u!   5 Me, Leslie, and Nechole.   6 I'm having a great time!   7 One of my best friends, Mike. Hugs and kisses.

1 My paternal grandmother, Annie Watkins.　2 Mom and me at the '96 Olympics in Atlanta.　3 Butchie.　4 Auntia Velva.　5 Family outing. 6 Uncles Victor and Quynton.　7 Cousin Nzinga and Aunt Venus.

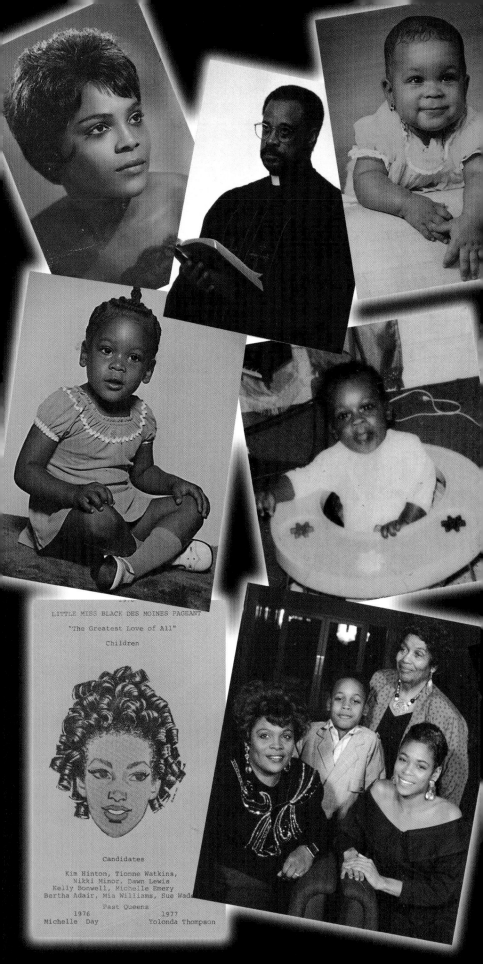

LITTLE MISS BLACK DES MOINES PAGEANT

"The Greatest Love of All"

Children

Candidates

Kim Hinton, Tionne Watkins,
Nikki Minor, Dawn Lewis
Kelly Bonwell, Michelle Emery
Bertha Adair, Mia Williams, Sue Wade

Past Queens
1976   1977
Michelle Day   Yolonda Thompson

1 My mom.   2 My dad, the reverend.   3 Me at six months.
4 My mom in her time and prime.   5 Wow! My mom, dad, and me
in Afro City.   6 Me at age four.   7 My baby brother.   8 My first
pageant.   9 Mom, Koko, Grandma, and me.   10 Renzy, me, Mela,
and Sky.   11 My mom and me at the "No Scrubs" shoot.

Ten Fan Questions

—from our contest winners

I'd like to thank each and every person who has written in a question, or sent some artwork or photographs to me. All these things really made me sit and think out my thoughts for this book, and the ten winners' questions helped to form the following essays. I hope they answer *all* your questions!

1. (A) **How do you deal with the pain of loss?**
   (B) **How did you become this strong person?**
   From: JL106785@aol.com
         Jenna Bryant

2. **Who has been an inspiration to you in your life besides your family?**
   From: KATAMOC@home.net
         Katy O'Connell

3. **How do you manage to survive in a world of fame and not much freedom?**
   From: MIVIDALOCA@theriver.com
         Daryla Quintana

4. **Where were you born and raised?**
   From: RCUSTOL@gl.umbc.edu
         Rowena Garcia Custodio

5. **How did you get together with the other girls to become an awesome girl group?**
   From: AALIYAH@powwowmail.com
         Holly Hawkins

6. **Describe your most memorable TLC experience and why.**
   From: NIKIBSB@yahoo.com
         Amethyst Jones

7. **Has growing up without a father made you more determined to make it in life?**
   From: SWEETBROTHA4U@hotmail.com
         Jamari Akil Douglas

8. **Is there any significant moment in your childhood that you can reflect on that has played a role in shaping the person that you are today?**
   From: LUVLANC3@aol.com
         Kim Demaddas

9. **What inspired you to write *Thoughts*?**
   From: KBANIS4979@blacktop.com
         Laree Banister

10. **What inspired you to write the song "Unpretty?"**
    From: DSHUM1@sprint.ca
          Serena Shum

Grandma Velma

The ride back home was a quiet one. Mom sat in the passenger seat looking out the window at the sun beginning to rise. I would glance over at her from the road every once in a while. I had run out of things to say. I had tried to make small talk to fill the silence but Momma wasn't paying much attention. She was exhausted; we both were. We had been at the hospital on and off for three days and then spent the night. I don't remember ever seeing my momma cry. Tonight, though, she shed tears; we both did. I focused on the driving, slowly winding through the streets of Atlanta. We would arrive at home and, for the first time, Grandma wouldn't be in the downstairs apartment. She was with God and in my heart, and I would have to get used to no longer being able to hug her or sing to her.

At home, the rest of the family began reassembling from the hospital—my aunts and uncles, my cousins. Gradually, we all ended up in Grandma's apartment, reminiscing, looking through the photos. We talked and laughed as we remembered and sometimes one of us would just cry all of a sudden. Everything caught up with me and I suddenly wanted to sleep, so I crawled into Grandma's bed. I embraced her pillow and breathed deep, taking her scent into my lungs. It was a warm smell, a smell that meant home to me.

When I was twelve years old, my mom and I moved in with Grandma. Mom was pregnant and felt it would be easier to have the baby back home in Des Moines, Iowa. I thought it was a great idea. Grandma was like a second mother to me and I loved being around her. Back when we had first moved to Atlanta, Georgia, I cried the whole way—not so much because I was leaving behind my friends and what I knew, but because I thought I'd never see Grandma again.

Living with her, I wanted to do everything she did. When she sat down to watch her soap operas I was right there next to her. We'd watch *The Young and the Restless*, *As the World Turns*, and *Guiding Light*. During the commercials we'd gossip and Grandma would fill me in on some background that I didn't know. I was hooked on the soaps for the next ten years and only gave them up when my schedule with TLC made it impossible to follow the programs. Grandma also enjoyed a good cup of coffee, which I could not understand. I hated it, but if Grandma liked it there had to be something good in it. So I'd take a little bit of coffee and add lots of cream to hide the taste and I'd feel like an adult sharing some downtime with her.

I never added milk to my coffee because I was allergic to it. Instead, I drank the powdered milk, Isomil, which is meant for babies. It tasted just plain nasty, and I tried to avoid drinking it when I could. But Grandma worked up a concoction with the powdered coffee creamer that made it sweeter and a lot more fun to drink.

Isomil, though, was nowhere as gross as Grandma's favorite sandwich. She just could not convince me that a peanut butter, jelly, and banana sandwich was any good. I tried it but just gave up, feeling like this was one thing I didn't have to do like Grandma. I mean, really, there's only so much a girl can do. I'd say, "Grandma, sorry, but that is nasty. I don't know how you eat it."

Now she didn't believe you should say that. She believed that you should appreciate the food you have. She'd say, "Tionne, food is not nasty." And I'd say, "But Grandma, it really is." She would smile at me then. I think I was the only one in the family who could get away with saying that about food.

After my brother Koko was born, Mom went back to Atlanta to find us a place to live, look for a job, and get everything set up. I stayed behind with Grandma for about a month. Grandma would get up every morning and make me eggs with bacon. I had a dog, Tishia, who would also join us for breakfast. Grandma would make him a special dish of eggs, too, and she'd add chunks of hot dogs. I can tell you that Tishia was one happy dog. I'd help clean up the kitchen, and then she'd go to work as a teacher at Tiny Tots, a nursery that was right across the street from her house. I'd go to school and one of my aunts would watch Koko.

It was during this time that I got my first period. I was totally scared by the blood and thought something was wrong with me. Grandma helped me through it, though, explaining what it was and how to deal with it. It brought us even closer.

Being a popular teacher and living near the school meant everyone knew Grandma's house—1601 Forest Avenue—especially around Christmastime. That was when she made her specialty, the most amazing fudge you will ever taste. The warm, sweet smell would fill the house and the family could not resist sneaking some of that fudge while it was still warm. Grandma would make batches for some people in the neighborhood and at the school, and she'd also send them out to relatives who weren't able to make it to her house. Whenever I smell fudge, it sends me back to those days when Grandma would come out of the kitchen with a platter full of it and they'd all pick it clean within minutes. We would sing Christmas songs, eat, sing some more, and eat some more. She would sit at the table, beaming. Those were some of her most happy times. She loved to hear her children gather and sing.

The first house I bought my mom in Atlanta.

I used to tell my grandma that if I ever made any money, I was going to buy her a place in Atlanta. After I had some success with TLC, I decided it was time to make good on my promise, especially since she had been suffering with pain. Her hips had deteriorated to a point where they had to be replaced. Mom would fly back and forth to care for her and periodically Grandma would go through the different stages of the hip replacement. I felt it would make it easier on both of them if Grandma just moved in with my mom.

But she was real stubborn and did not want to leave Des Moines. I understood that. She had spent a lifetime there, raising her nine children, being a part of the community. It was everything she knew. She wasn't getting any younger, though—she was in her early eighties—and Mom and I decided moving her to Atlanta was the best thing.

We had a four-bedroom house built with a downstairs that had a two-bedroom apartment with a big living room, den, and kitchen. When it was done we convinced Grandma to fly in. Once we got home, I was so excited. I brought her downstairs, showed it to her and said, "Grandma, we built this for you." She saw that we were serious, and she was too practical to turn down a spacious apartment that was built just for her. Still, she was a stubborn and independent woman and it took some discussion before she finally agreed to move in. I was thrilled. She felt she'd live like a queen with all the space and the convenience of having the family around. I was so happy to have kept my promise.

She moved to Atlanta on Thanksgiving Day, 1997. She was feeling better after the hip surgery and the physical therapy. After she moved in, she did indeed live like a queen; she got a couple good months in and it felt like everything would be okay. When she fell sick again she underwent a series of exams. Eventually the doctors diagnosed her with uterine cancer, which would spread to her lungs. Over the course of 1998, Mom would take care of her, taking her to the doctors and the treatments, day in and day out.

In early October, they put a hospital bed in Mom's living room. The cancer had gotten to a point where they couldn't do anything more in the hospital. They felt she was better off being home around her family. We were glad to have her home, and home was where she wanted to be. But no one was happy about handling the medical stuff. A nurse trained my mom and aunts on how to hook up the IV, give her medicines, and that sort of thing. It was a scary time for everyone in the family because you couldn't make mistakes. If you didn't hook up the IV right and air got in the tubing, she could die. Who knew what would happen if you gave her the wrong dosage or combinations of medication? No one wanted that kind of responsibility. Doctors and nurses, they're paid professionals who do this for a living. What did we know? It was upsetting, and some of my aunts and uncles wouldn't touch the IV. Still, everyone took shifts and did what they could. It was up to us and we weren't going to let down this woman we all loved.

Because of my TLC obligations, I couldn't tend to Grandma, though I really wanted to. I would visit whenever I could, to sit with her, even if it was when she was sleeping. She had gotten tiny over time. She was not a tall woman, she was about five-three, but she was solid and strong. With the chemotherapy, though, she had lost her hair and much of her weight. The IV kept her hydrated and made up for her lack of appetite, because the chemo made it hard for her to keep anything down. She couldn't stand certain smells either; she was extra-sensitive to some that would literally make her sick.

I remember visiting her once; she was sitting on the couch, tiny like a little baby bird. She didn't care for wearing a wig in the house, though sometimes she'd wear one when we went out on those days when she had been better. I looked at her this one day and it amazed me how beautiful she looked, with no wrinkles even at eighty-three. "Grandma, you're really pretty," I said.

"Oh dear, you've got to be kidding me," she said, not agreeing with me at all.

"No, really. You're face is flawless. It's clear. So what if you're smaller. Your face is so pretty, Grandma." I think it made her made her feel a little better.

That's not to say she would take any sympathy from me. She said I had been a sickly child, and I had lived with all the IVs and what not. I said, "Your disease is way worse than mine, Grandma, I don't think there's any comparison."

"Pain is pain," she told me with a shrug.

When she was going through the chemo treatments I came out and asked her, "Are you going to give up or are you going to keep fighting it? Are you gonna hold on?"

"What do you think? I'm going to fight it, sweetie. I'm never going to give up," she said. She stayed positive, with a smile on her face, this eighty-three–year-old woman whose body was failing her. No matter how she was feeling, she would give me pep talks. Watching her deal with her illness and impending death taught me a lot about how to live. Not until the pain had gotten insufferable and she was at death's door did she ever seem like the cancer was going to bring her down emotionally or mentally. Her struggle proved her strength and it truly inspired me. It made my own day-to-day problems seem insignificant, and whenever I have a sickle cell crisis, I'll tough it out like Grandma would have.

Just before Halloween I got the flu and couldn't be around her because the chemo and the medications had thrown her immune system out of whack. I did stay at my mom's house though, which is where I am whenever I'm sick. There she can keep an eye on me because she doesn't think I'm responsible enough to take care of myself. If it were up to me, I'd get up and do the things I need to do, regardless of how I felt. But at Mom's I feel calm and grounded, and she makes sure I stay that way.

Grandma's last few days were hard ones. She was almost delirious with pain. I really wanted her to listen to the cuts from *Fanmail* before it was too late. But she couldn't bring herself to focus enough to listen to much of anything, much less to the album. Before I went to bed on Halloween night, I put on a germ mask so I could say good night. She seemed so tired and upset, in a way that I'd never seen before. My Uncle Quynton was holding and hugging her. I couldn't get too close to her because of the virus, so I just called out to her and hoped she could hear me.

My housewarming party in Atlanta in 1997.

In the middle of the night someone woke me up and said Grandma was breathing funny. We called the ambulance and went to the hospital. We didn't want her to die at the house. Maybe there was something that could be done at the hospital, after all. But the doctors said there was nothing they could do but wait. They changed her into a hospital gown and gave her painkillers so she could be comfortable, then they moved her from the emergency room to a private room. She fell into a coma. A minister showed up and gave her last rites and stayed around to give us comfort.

But my grandma wouldn't go down so easy. She was so strong that she brought herself out of the coma like she wanted to tell us something. She said, "Someone please let me out of here. I want to go home."

When she lapsed back into the coma, we would put the phone to her ear so people could say their last words to her. She would make a sound to acknowledge what someone said, so I knew she was able to hear what we were saying and singing to her.

I was watching a movie about the Temptations in the waiting room when my Aunt Ressie came out and told us Grandma was starting to slip away. We went in and formed a circle around the bed and started singing to her again. The nurses there started crying; they said they'd never heard a family singing at someone's deathbed. But this was our tribute to her, something that would ease her journey to the other side, surrounded by love. There were my mom's sisters, Sandra, Ressie, Karen, and Venus. My two cousins, Marde and Nzinga, and my Aunt Sandra and Uncle Jeff had just left. My brother Koko was home. He had just turned sixteen, and my mom didn't want him to see this.

One of Grandma's favorite songs was "Jesus Loves Me," and my mom sang it to her with her sisters. I joined in with them even though I just wanted to stand and listen to the voices of these women gathered like angels around the bed of their mother.

Grandma was struggling with her breathing. My mom held her hand and whispered to her, "Go ahead, Momma, and rest. Let it go. Don't fight it." Grandma took two breaths, then one deep breath. She went limp and her head fell to the side. I was standing behind my mom with my hand on her shoulder and my other hand on Grandma's leg. We continued to sing for a little while longer, then we all started crying and hugging one another.

It was 1:34 in the morning. We stayed in the room. It was difficult leaving Grandma's body. Some of us would talk to her as if she were still there. Then my Aunt Velva and Uncle Quynton arrived, and that was hard for them. It made everyone cry again.

Still, we all knew that God was going to take care of Grandma. She was a good Christian woman who had raised a loving family.

Over the next few days we had the wake, which I didn't go to. I didn't want to see her like that more than once, and I knew I would see her at the funeral. We took her home to Iowa to be buried.

I miss her. But in my heart I know Velma Coleman didn't die. She simply lives in a better place, where she can watch over her family.

From Des Moines to the Dirty South

Christmas at an Atlanta shelter.

Moving to Atlanta from Des Moines was a nightmare. I cried the whole way, "I don't wanna go, I don't wanna go!" We were leaving behind Grandma, family, everyone and everything I had ever known. You'd think driving through Illinois, Missouri, Kentucky, and Tennessee on a thousand-mile trip would be an adventure for a kid. But for me it was the longest ride of my life.

My mom is a get-up-and-go woman and she had no problems just picking up and leaving a place she had lived all her life for what she thought was something better. I think for her the south was someplace romantic and nostalgic. And I think she was plain tired of the midwest and already knew what it had to offer. The south, well, it was up to her to see what to make of it. Now, I should say she didn't even know anyone in Atlanta, which was scary to me. For Mom, it was taking her nine-year-old girl and striking out on her own. For me, it was just plain crazy.

Especially after what we'd just been through in Houston, Texas, my mom's first choice of a southern town.

I can't remember a single good thing that happened to us the nine months we were in Houston. We had some serious bad luck. My mom found a two-bedroom apartment in Houston that was not as big as our three-story house at 2030 High Street in Des Moines. Mom worked three jobs to get us ready for the move, buying new furniture so it'd be a real fresh start. We hired a moving company and they loaded up the tractor-trailer. The plan was they would get a head start and we would meet them down in Houston. A couple of days later, we got a call from the moving company: The truck had been vandalized and burned.

We got in the car and Mom drove in a hurry. By the time we arrived, it was all a smoldering mess. We weren't able to go into the trailer, but it was easy to see that it was mostly empty. The nicest pieces of furniture, the television and stereo, we didn't see any of it. As hard as it was to believe, the driver and his partner had taken what they wanted then set fire to everything else. It was bad enough they had stolen from us, but then they had to destroy everything else we owned? All we had left were some clothes in the suitcases sitting in the trunk of the car. My mom was devastated, but we couldn't prove any of it. Instead of a happy new beginning, we had to start from scratch.

We did our best to settle in. Soon after, we got into a car accident. Our little Volkswagen got totaled by a Cadillac. So now we had no clothes, no furniture, and no car. Still, Mom was going to stick it out. My mom, always looking out for the less fortunate no matter how badly things were going for us, took this poor kid Vincent under her wing. He was my age, and we'd have him over to our house where he'd spend time, hang out, eat. He seemed like a nice enough kid until I came home one day and found my piggy bank gone. Now this wasn't any small piggy bank. No, Mom was saving coins like silver dollars and some gold coins, too, for my college tuition. (Little did she know I wasn't really interested in going to college, but that's beside the point!) Vincent had stolen hundreds of dollars worth of the coins. I don't know what he planned on doing with that money, but my mom wasn't going to let him get away with it.

When we pulled up in front of his apartment, Mom said, "You stay here." I sat tight in the car while she talked to Vincent's mother, then confronted him. But it was too late; only a few coins were left. We were very disappointed in him and never saw him again.

Not too long after, we heard about a three-year-old child who had her neck slit around the corner from our house. Then mom was five minutes late picking me up from school. She found a man trying to lure me into his car. All this and a couple of sickle-cell crises thrown in and that was enough to say goodbye to Houston.

We moved to California for about six months so Mom could look after one of my aunts who became ill. Our time there was a blur to me, and after going back to Des Moines for a little bit, we moved to the "dirty south," Atlanta. This time we were joined by Mom's best friend, Una May, who left her husband. She took her daughter Tae Tae with her.

We arrived in Atlanta in the fall, still without much furniture, so we had to improvise. For our first Thanksgiving at our new apartment in Union City we set up cardboard boxes, then covered them with a sheet to make a pretty table. Then the four of us had some turkey, biscuits, gravy, collard greens. It was beginning to feel like home.

It didn't take me long to realize that Atlanta was the bomb, that if my mom hadn't left Des Moines, I would have scratched out on my own. Watching television and seeing what was going on in the world showed me that there was so much going on, and you could only catch it in bigger cities. There just wasn't enough in Des Moines to hold me down. In Atlanta you'll find the latest culture has to offer—the hippest clothes, the latest movies, dance styles ahead of everyone's time. Atlanta is also cool because I can get away in minutes to the pretty suburbs with the quiet and the trees. I also love Atlanta because it gets hot. The cold makes me achy and, fortunately, it's not cold too often down here. I love the vibe here, too. I can go around the corner to the grocery store to run an errand and I don't have to be dressed up like you have to be in Los Angeles, where everyone's a star. I also don't have to wear a disguise, like Michael Jackson. Here there are country home-grown people and they leave you to yourself.

Of course, there are still things I miss about Iowa: seeing all my aunts and uncles more regularly, being around my cousins, and the food. In Des Moines, it is off the hook. There you'll find these really big beef or pork tenderloin sandwiches at Millie's Tenderloins. They are the biggest, juiciest, tastiest sandwiches you will ever eat, and they are addictive. In fact, I've got some frozen in my fridge right now. At Mustard's they had sugar biscuits—biscuits fried and dipped in sugar—that tasted a little like donuts but they were like chewing on little pieces of heaven. Then at Tasty Taco you'll find the best tacos in the country. The shell is soft and breadlike and the filling is just amazing. Just the other day my mom brought home twenty Tasty Tacos, which we ate in two days. When Mom goes to Des Moines to visit family, she makes a point of picking up some of my favorite foods and bringing them home to me.

Koko

A couple years later, Mom got pregnant and we moved back to Des Moines so we could live with Grandma, and Mom could have the baby. To tell the truth, I had no idea what was going to happen. I knew she was pregnant, but I didn't realize what that meant: that this little life would be born and that he would change all our lives. I was fine with the way things were. Over the course of my life, I may have wondered what it'd be like to have an older brother or sister (Mom had two miscarriages), but I never really longed for it. I wanted my mom all to myself anyway.

I was a little jealous when Koko was born. I was my mommy's little girl, twelve years old, spoiled, an only child who was usually the center of attention. To me he was a thing that came home and stole the spotlight. When Mom came from the hospital with the little bundle in her arms, everyone in the family would come visit and fawn over him. They would take turns holding him, telling stories about their own babies and their own childbirth experiences. I felt that I was left to myself. I would wonder when he was going back and finally my mom told me he was here to stay. There wasn't much else to do then but accept my baby brother Koko. Before long, I loved him and became like a second mother to him. When Mom worked nights at UPS, I would cook my brother dinner, help him with his homework, and put him to bed. And not for once do I look at him as my half-brother. My father's kids, I see them as my half-brothers, because they have a different mother. But for me and Koko, we come from the same womb and share the same mother. We're blood. Nothing will ever change that.

He's sixteen now, but I'm still telling him what he should and shouldn't do. Sometimes he comes and stays with me and I take him on some of my business trips. I recently took him with me to L.A., and had him fly back by himself, which made me completely paranoid. He may be a big boy to some people (he's 6'1" and weighs about 220 pounds), but he's a baby to me. So I had to have someone not only bring him to the airport but also make sure he got on the plane. Then in Atlanta I had someone pick him up at the gate and walk him to the car. I will pass out if he gets lost and something goes wrong. "Here's the cell phone," I told him before he left, "and here's some money in case anything goes wrong." Then I worried until Mom called me to say he got home okay.

Koko wants to try his hand at producing. He comes over to my studio and makes beats. He's actually getting pretty good, and I'm thinking I may sell a couple tracks for him so he can put some money in the bank. As much as I want to spoil him, he has to learn that I'm not going to buy him a new pair of Jordans whenever they come out. I would love to buy him a car, but I want him to save up money for car insurance. That'll be something he'll have to handle on his own. I'm really trying to teach him responsibility, the necessity of having a job, and the importance of education.

Koko's in high school right now and he's going to college whether he likes it or not. There's a chance he might be able to get a sports scholarship because he's a great baseball player. He's been playing T-ball since he was four, and he's got all kinds of trophies. As a child he always took the game seriously, never showing up late to a game, always on the practice field, and he'd get mad at the whole team if they'd do something stupid to lose. Still, scholarship or not, it's important to me and to my mother that he go to college. Even if he ends up as an athlete or a music producer, it's good to have a plan B or plan C to fall back on. Nothing's promised, and an education is never wasted.

Yes, there are exceptions. When you hear about guys like Bill Gates, the richest guy on the planet, who is a college dropout, you think, hey, he didn't need it. But for people like Gates, it's not because he was lazy or had nothing going on, and success just landed in his lap. He was pursuing his passion. He was on the cutting edge of his business. He was teaching himself, working hard and, with some luck, good things happened for him. No one should expect that can happen for them. My mom believes that and is hard on my brother because, as a man, not only will he have to look after himself, but he'll also have to take care of a wife and children one day. A woman can marry a man who has money and be okay for the rest of her life. But, nine times out of ten, a man can't marry a woman who has money and have her taking care of him.

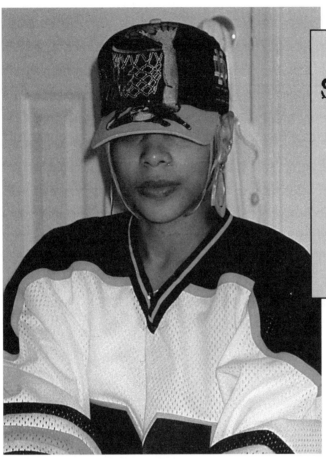

High
School:
The
Worst
Years
of My
Life

After reading about how important I think education is, you might think I just loved going to school. You'd be wrong. I had all kinds of problems in high school and it really put a strain on my relationship with my mom.

When I was in Iowa I went to St. Theresa's, a nice white Catholic school. Mom sent me there not because we were Catholic, but because she felt I'd get a better education than at a public school. I did well there, got good grades, and everything was pretty normal. Things changed, though, once we were back in Atlanta, having moved back with my baby brother Koko.

From the seventh until tenth grades I was very angry. I just became mad at everybody and very rebellious. It wouldn't take much for me to get into a fight because I had a hair-trigger temper. I also liked to be with people who were just as stupid and ignorant as I was, which didn't help the situation. I didn't like girls, so I hung out with guys. These weren't your nice, quiet types of guys. They were street, troublemakers who wouldn't think twice about protecting me or picking a fight. After school, we'd get into fights with anyone and everyone. Thing was, because of the sickle cell anemia, if someone punched me hard enough, I would go into a crisis and that would put me in the hospital where I'd get really sick. But I'd fight anyway. I didn't think I was abnormal as a child or that I should have any special treatment. If you're born with something and you've lived your whole life like that, you don't think you're different until you go into the outside world and say, you all don't drink baby milk, you can eat ice cream, you can go swimming in the water when it's cold? I didn't know any better. Thankfully, I didn't get beat up.

Grades, attendance, homework, these were the last things on my mind. I just did not care about applying myself. I got an F for gym because I wouldn't dress up. It's not that I couldn't do well, it's that I didn't want to. It's no surprise then that I scored plenty of Fs with a few Ds. And the other students were not the only targets of this anger I couldn't contain. I'd cuss out all the teachers, not wanting to hear what they had to say, and I'd leave the classroom whenever I wanted to. I had a problem with authority figures and people telling me what to do. I would say, "You're not my mother or father, you don't put a roof over my head or feed me. How can you tell me to shut up? You want to remix that?" If you didn't respect me I was not going to respect you. Back then I didn't realize I wasn't acting in a way that would demand anyone's respect, particularly a teacher's.

So here's a big shock: I got kicked out of four schools. I was practically a delinquent! Things got so bad that I was blacklisted and none of the other schools in the county would take me. My mom then made arrangements to have me bused out to a school in Fairburn. It was a thirty-minute bus ride each way, and I wasn't having any of that. I didn't care what my mom had gone through to get me into that school, or that my options were running out. I made some hell there, too, and soon got expelled. That's when all the talking stopped.

Until then, my mom had tried to understand. We would talk about why I was angry, what was going on in my head. For me, it all seemed to stem from my anger at my dad. The feelings of abandonment and being unloved were not something I knew how to deal with. All I could dwell on were the negatives, not the fact that I still had a loving mother and a cute little baby brother who loved me unconditionally. No, lashing out at the world and taking it down with me were all I was thinking about. Now, though, Mom was tired of all the mind games.

She grabbed me by my shirt, her hands balled up into fists. She said, "Now I'm going to beat you down. I will knock you out. You are going to graduate. You are going to get a diploma. You are going to finish high school. You are going to stop this!" She was not fooling. So after she found another school that was willing to accept me, I started eleventh grade. The next two years killed me. Teachers would say things to me and I would just put my head down. It would eat me up because I couldn't stand it when people got smart with me. But I would put up with it because I didn't want my momma to beat me down. That girl could fight! Heck, I remember once when these girls wanted to jump me. I asked my mom, "Mom, you gonna come to school to help me fight?" I figured, who better? She started laughing and told me I should just stay home. No way was I going to do that. Then they'd think I was scared. I'd rather go get beat down than have them think that. Nothing came of it, though it would've been cool to see my mom and me taking those girls on.

At my new school, I scored a few As and Bs as I paid a little more attention. But, really, some of the stuff they were teaching was beyond me—like algebra and geometry. I always wanted to be an entertainer, and I had no idea what any of that had to do with my career plans or my personal life. I used to sit in those classes, thinking, "Why am I here?" What, I'll be shopping in the mall and tell a salesperson, "Y plus ten equals two to the tenth power, can I have my shirt please?" To this day, I've never used algebra or geometry.

I did enjoy other classes, especially the creative ones like art, and band, where I played the clarinet. Classes like that seemed more relevant and meaningful to me.

Still, as usual, I had to go for an extra six weeks of classes in summer school. I was Watkins sitting in the back, and I was like, "Can you bore me any more than this?" I did manage to finish and get my diploma, even though, because of summer school, I had to graduate in '89 with people I didn't know. At the ceremony, I don't know if I felt any sense of pride or accomplishment. It was more that I was just glad it was over and I could get on with my life. Today I appreciate having that diploma more than I did then, thanks to Mom. Everything she did for me, whether it made me mad or not, has helped me as an adult. As a teen, I just didn't understand. She disciplined me and stayed on top of me and I needed that.

Mom, of course, wanted me to go to college. At first I wanted to go to the School of Art and Design in New York City to be a fashion designer. I begged to go for about a year and a half. Finally, at graduation she told me I could go, but by then I didn't want to anymore. I didn't want to leave home. With Mom's voice in my ear, I was then thinking of getting an associate's degree. I figured that if I didn't become a successful entertainer I should have something to fall back on. But I had no desire to go to college. I just knew it would be a waste of my time and her money. So I decided on vocational school.

Get a J-O-B

At beauty school I specialized in nails. I didn't see myself doing it forever; at that age who thinks that far ahead? I liked doing it and I could control it by working my own hours, making my own money, and being my own boss. I wanted to do what I wanted to do; I didn't want anyone ordering me around. I guess that's pretty obvious now, but it really hit home during my first job at McDonald's. That was a place I'd rather eat at than work in.

Everything was going fine at the golden arches until the manager asked me to wash the windows. I said, "No, thank you. I don't wash windows." She even asked me to clean up the tables and sweep the floor. I was like, "Do what?" When I first started, I thought I would give away free food to my friends and work the drive-through, spread the joyous message of Ronald McDonald and make children of all ages smile. Then when it came to this cleaning business, I said, "Wait a minute. For $3.25? I don't think so." I don't think I lasted more than two weeks there.

My second job was at a beauty supply store, which I enjoyed. I worked behind the counter, operating the cash register. A big-time drug dealer owned the place and he was nice enough to pay us in cash in a pink envelope, tax-free! It's also where I met my friend Rico Wade, who changed my life by helping TLC get together. He also was responsible for my first makeover. Back in those days I used to dress like a girl and one day he gave me a present, my first pair of baggy jeans. When I first tried them on, they fell to my ankles. I was like, "I don't understand how you make them stay up." He put a belt through the loops and made it hang off my butt just so. Then he stepped back, looked me over, and said, "You phat!" I was like, "Word? Okay, I got it." It took me a little while to get used to walking with those big pants, but from then on I dressed like a boy.

I then got a job as a shampoo assistant at a hair salon. That's where I met Marie, who now does hair for TLC and who introduced us to Pebbles. Eventually, I became an apprentice for hair under a guy named Maurice. But things didn't work out too well there. I brought my attitude problem into the salon and thought, "Whatever." I didn't like girls, so maybe a beauty salon wasn't the best place for me to be working, and I didn't care about the owner or the fact that this was her salon. At one point she asked me to work under her, but I said no, thinking that she just wanted me to kiss up to her. Anyway,

Me with everyone who helped out at the signing.

things got progressively worse after that, and on my last day there, the owner called the police, fired me, and kicked me out. I was really hurt by that. Instead of just telling me I was out of a job, she went through this whole drama and humiliated me.

I later met up with the owner when I was in beauty school. She paid the rest of my tuition, bought me supplies, and hired me at her new store. She never explained why she did it; maybe that was her way of saying sorry. I was happy to put into practice what I was learning, so I took the job. When I started doing nails really well and fast, I felt like I didn't need to be at the school anymore. I had learned about all the types of nail fungi and all that, and I was getting bored. I figured I had conquered it and there was no need to study anymore. I was ready to work full-time at the salon, but the teacher wanted me to read a book. I, of course, refused, and I stopped showing up regularly. The course lasted six weeks and I went maybe three weeks. I still was able to get my certificate, though, because I had on-the-job training at the salon.

I was doing nails during the day and also got a night job telemarketing, where I hustled to sell. I didn't mind the hard work, and I needed the money to buy things for myself and make the load easier on my mom. I was about eighteen and my mom was telling me I needed to start being responsible for myself and figure out what I was going to do. She told me that the one mistake she made was spoiling me too much. She said, "I've got to make you more responsible because if I put you out in the world like that, you wouldn't know what to do."

Up until then, I had never gone to a store to buy clothes for myself. And even if I did, I wouldn't have known my size—not my panties, bras, pants, shirts, nothing. Mom did all my clothes shopping. When I was in school, she would lay out my clothes on the bed, underwear and socks or hosiery included. Not only did I not buy the clothes, but I didn't take care of them, either. And my mom had had enough of that. "I am sick of seeing all your clothes on the floor. That's it, sister. I ain't buying nothing no more." It was time for me to buy the things I needed for myself. Mom always believed you should have things that you own, whether it be a television, a house, or a car. Always have your own, she would tell me, because even if you get married, your husband could die or up and leave you—anything could happen, so make your own nest. Take care of yourself and don't depend on someone else.

She was telling this to someone who at eighteen didn't know how to go to the doctor and fill out forms. I needed to learn how to handle things on my own. It was time to grow up and be a woman.

I went to Maple Street Baptist Church every Sunday when I was a kid. In my family, you had to. And we wouldn't just dress up pretty and sit in the back pew of the church. No, we were part of the service. My mom was in a singing group called the Viduelles, and her song was "Going Over Yonder." My mom was the jam in church, the one who had the big song that would get everyone jumping and crying. Her voice would make everything feel bigger and you'd swear you were being filled with the spirit. I would watch her in amazement as she got worked up, relishing each note that escaped her lips.

Unfortunately, I couldn't just watch her sing. I was in the children's choir and would have to sing "You're Gonna Be Sorry." Every Wednesday we would go to choir practice, but I didn't really enjoy it, mostly because I didn't have a name back then. No one would call me Tionne, only Little Gayle. "Oh come here, Little Gayle, you so cute, you look just like your momma." I didn't want to be the "Little Gayle" singing. I'd rather just watch my mom sing.

If you were to see my mom and me together, there'd be no mistaking that I am my mother's daughter. I have her eyes, eyebrows, nose, smile. Her face is a little darker and way thicker because I didn't get all her booty. My mom's very pretty, so when people say

I look like her, I'm flattered. We've been through a lot together, good times and bad, and she has taught me everything I know about being human.

When I was in high school, Mom once owned a gray Oldsmobile that looked like a big battleship. I was so embarrassed by it that I used to tell her not to drop me off in front of school where all the other kids could see us. She would tell me I shouldn't be ashamed of anything I had, and then she would pull up right in front of the school where all of God's children could see us. "Girl," my mom would say, "you better be proud of what you have. We're lucky we even have a car. We're having hard times right now."

I got the message. It was a difficult time for us because we had just moved back to Atlanta and Koko was still a toddler. My mom was working different jobs to make ends meet. There were nights when we would eat popcorn or watermelon for dinner because we didn't have any money. Sometimes we'd have to roll up pennies to go get some food. She always made sure we ate. A couple of times we just had to make sure we had the money to pay rent and it meant not buying new clothes. But we always had a roof over our head and clothes on our back.

Once we were on our feet again, we had to deal with the usual craziness. As with Vincent in Houston, my mother had no problem helping people who were less fortunate than we were. Most people were grateful for the kindness and would be able to get themselves together and move on. But not everyone. One time a cousin with a serious crack problem stayed over. Soon enough, a silver set that was given by a relative who had passed on was missing. He never copped to it, but it didn't matter. It was gone and there was nothing we could do to replace something so sentimental. There were other incidents, too, of TVs, VCRs, and other things stolen by our own people, but I don't want to get into that. It's too upsetting. There was one other incident that I could not believe. One of my friends once stole all my clothes—my panties, bras—as well as my diamond earrings.

People have told me I have a big heart, and I do trust people to a certain extent. I also have no problem giving the shirt off my back to help somebody. But when you steal from me, look out. When this girl took these personal things from me, I wanted to go after her, but Mom chimed in with her "two wrongs don't make a right." But I was seeing red. I went to my so-called friend's house, confronted her, and took my stuff back. We got into a fight and I came out on top. Then I took some of her things to show her what it felt like. My mom was mad at me, but what did she expect? She took my clothes and jewelry! I couldn't let that go. I was the victim, not her. Why should I feel sorry for someone who steals from my house? I opened my home to you, fed you, let you sleep in my house, gave you money when you were broke, and you steal from me? Well then, I'm going to your house and I'm going to take what I think you owe me. My mom made me give it back, which made me angry, but I did it anyway. I did beat the girl up, and that made me feel better. The next time yet another friend stole from me, my mom did talk me out of beating her up. I didn't feel good about it, but letting it go was probably best. It just ate at me to think this girl got over on me. Mom was right, though. She said, "Don't be vindictive or bitter. Get that off your heart because it hurts no one else but you." She made me understand you reap what you sow. Mom would also try to make me feel better by saying things like, "The girl knows she can't mess with you. You know you could beat her up." Mom knew how to talk to me!

So you can see why Mom and I are always there for each other. If I have problems with some knucklehead boyfriend and it's Valentine's Day, it doesn't matter. I know Mom will have chocolate or a card for me. I know she's going to have something to make me smile no matter who's done me wrong.

To this day, every Easter I get a different stuffed bunny rabbit and a basket from my mom. This year I got a bunny whose cheeks light up and he laughs and talks. I've got a whole collection of stuffed animals in my house's kiddie room. They bring a smile to my face whenever I look in there. I told Mom she could only stop giving me the bunnies after I got married. I don't think she minds.

Growing up, Easter was a special holiday for the family. Mom used to dress me up in a pretty outfit she bought just for the occasion, and then we'd go to church. Afterward, we'd have a big lunch with the family, color eggs, and have an egg hunt. But, really, the biggest holiday was Christmas. Mom would go all out for that.

She would clear all the furniture out of the living room and put in a baby roller coaster and a little carousel. It was like a little amusement park in the house. I'd get really big gifts. My favorite gift ever was a pink Huffy bike. I rode that bike all over the neighborhood and when the training wheels came off, that was a big day! Mom, my cousin, and my uncle watched me ride away all by myself. Mom followed me the first few steps, afraid I'd fall over, but soon enough I was streaking down the sidewalk.

My gifts to my mom and relatives weren't nearly as nice. I used to find things around the house and wrap them up like new, or make cards, or write songs and poems. I didn't have any money so I would just make these creative little things that would make me feel like I was giving something back.

The holiday parties were either at my grandma's house or my mom's house or both, where you'd have dinner at one and coffee and dessert at the other. Now we have them at my house or my mom's place. We try and get as much family as possible together and spend the night before baking, cooking, and singing. It's a fun and special time for all of us.

And now that I'm hosting some of the holiday parties, I realize that just as my grandmother and mother used to share those responsibilities, I now share them with my mother. It's a passing on of a tradition that I truly cherish, especially now that I'm in a place where I can provide for my family.

My mom's last job was as a UPS truck driver, delivering boxes. I made her stop working because she damaged her back, and I had promised myself that if I ever had enough money, I would have her take a break, and if anyone deserves one, she does. But she's also very independent, and no matter how much money I make in life I cannot make my mother stop selling purses. She buys them wholesale, then turns around and sells them at retail to family, friends, neighbors, whoever she can get a hold of. Money or not, she's going to do it because she enjoys it. She does some interior decorating, too, sometimes for free. For a couple of years she also worked for LaFace Records to make their Christmas baskets.

I also buy her things to make her life easier. The first big gift I ever got her was a black Jeep. I drove up to her house and told her to come to the door. At first she thought I was showing her my new wheels, and then she realized it was for her. She was shocked and thought I was crazy. I think she felt funny accepting it at first, but after I worked on her for a little while, she didn't have any choice but to get behind the wheel and go for a drive. I've also bought her a house, and I plan on doing a whole lot more for her.

Right now I'm working on getting my mom a new home. Grandma's death had a huge effect on her. She has lupus, and being stressed out makes her achy and feverish. After Grandma's death, she was depressed and I thought that a new place, without the reminder of Grandma's downstairs apartment, may help her recover. She doesn't mope or anything, but deep down I know it eats at her every day. I think she does want to move but doesn't want me to go to any trouble. But she's got to realize by now that there isn't anything in the world I wouldn't do for her. She's everything to me.

Mom, I love you!

the voice

THE

do you hear things,
and they're only in your head?
look around, no one else hears them
hoping it's the good voice instead

people who say things
like someone told me to do it
do you think they're insane
or the voice drove them to it?

some are telling the truth
those stories are not lies
confiding in you may be
a way for you to hear their cries

don't give in to weakness
understand what you hear
your conscience won't lead you wrong
know the bad voice is not sincere

help those who can't help themselves
some hear things, they really do
don't judge, be supportive
you never know that person could be you

weight

weight is our size
but what does it mean?
how people judge us
if we're too fat or too lean

loss of weight
should be done for one's self
being anorexic or bulimic
is not good for your health

if someone threatens to leave you
because *they* feel your weight is wrong
they're not worthy of having you
subtract the negativity, leave them, be strong

everything's always easier said than done
showing that person your confidence
is how to get even, then yes you've won

life is too short
love yourself no matter what
never hate
don't let life pass you
worrying about your weight

what is a man
we'd all like to know
most men i know
have all been hoes

parenthood

what is a father?
who donates only semen
does not help his family
never around when
you need him

the ability to have children
doesn't make a good parent
it was just sex
meant nothing
now her face is transparent

what about that child
and how will he or she learn?
hopefully through a good mother
these days that's hard to earn

then we wonder
how that child got to be
don't you get it
don't you see

open your eyes

does it

Racism

racism is real
a touchy subject
i must admit
so as much as i can
i stay away from that shit

if someone doesn't like
my color of skin
when we jump out
we're all the same within

if all blood is red
and all humans die
the color of skin
shouldn't make a dif'
if so then why

all humans go to heaven
or even to hell
if color makes you trip
i can only say oh well
god bless you!

really matter?

tears

tears are water of sorrow
tears are water of joy

liquids of emotion
hate, love, happiness,
fear, plot, or ploy

crying can release things
sometimes crying is good
at times it's a feeling
that doesn't feel that good

but for whatever sad reasons
your tears may flow
i hope it releases some tension
for a better tomorrow

someone once
said something to me
that made me think
and the thought was
deep and actually
started to sink

you

if someone can't
be around for the
bad times they
shouldn't be around
for the good

and i thought
about that in a way
i never thought i would

when you're down
that's when people
are needed most

some people i couldn't
beg to be
there in spirit
even as my ghost

don't kick me down
when i'm already low

you'd think if
they cared
they'd automatically know

it makes you want
to define love
and what does
love mean

people use the word
but can't define what it means

but yet i put people first
and before myself
but not anymore
because now comes
my health

i have put aside
the things people do
not caring to have my back
made me take a second look at you

you who can't
feel what i go through
you who would
feel what i
feel if i were you

you who only
cares about yourself
you who doesn't
take time to think
of no one else

time brings on
a change
and my minutes
are better as time
goes on
and i hope you don't
reap for doing others wrong

you may not see it as anything
but right
but i have
to ask myself
how do you
sleep at night

celebrities

what makes you better
stars are in the sky
and when they're not happy
they often wonder why

just stay humble
that would be best
you can lose everything
and be laid to rest

money is material
and can't buy love
fans don't worship,
humans are not man above

celebrities are on tv and radio
just to entertain
celebs please don't forget
where you come from
and just remain the same

get a JOB

you won't get a job
and because of what
oh simply because you're content
sitting on your butt?

it's the same excuse
the lazy syndrome
you don't pay for nothing
and someone's house is home

uncle sam knows no color
let's just be for real
you live off people
that's easier than paying bills

god giveth and
god taketh away
if you were handicapped
you'd work a job any day

crime

what makes a man
turn to a life of crime
people with no arms or legs
wish they could work just one time

lots of things are tempting
we'd all like to steal
now you're charged with two crimes
'cause crime made you kill

you're doing exactly
what the devil wants you to
you reap what you sow
now tell me who's the fool

most times in crime
you'll always get caught
look down through history
and let the lesson be taught

who knew i'd be born
to become what i am
i'm good at my job
and it's not illegal nor a scam

it doesn't cost anything
to do what i do
although some think i'm stupid
and look like a fool

i don't ask for much
so don't call me names
i can't do it alone
and men will be the same

how can you just blame me
i just stand around
then here come the dogs
sniffing on my ground

and if it weren't for men
being as simple as they are
how could everyone know me
you all made me the star

TLC: Three Girls, One Dream

The early days of TLC were some of the best times we ever had, especially during the recording of the first album. We were working with Dallas Austin at Doppler Studios in Atlanta. We were so hyped putting all the tracks down, and had so much nervous energy between sessions that we would get a little wild. I'm not talking drinking, drugs, or sex. Nope, I'm talking about the most intense food fights you have ever seen. We would throw mustard, ketchup, water, sandwiches—you name it, we threw it.

One night we had a food fight that started in the control room and went through the whole building. It all began when the girls and I wanted revenge on Dallas for the last food fight we lost. Lisa mixed flour and water in a bowl, and the plan was to dump the whole mess on his head so it would run down his face and neck. But Lisa mixed it too thick. Instead of running down his face, the dough just stuck inside the bowl once we plopped it on his head. It messed up his hair a little, but it didn't do the necessary damage. Boy, did he get us back. Every time we would try to throw something at him, he would take our hands and make us mash ourselves in the face. Things escalated from there so that before you knew it, we were dumping water bottles on each other, chasing Dallas through the studio. We messed that studio up bad. There were pools of water in the hallways, and the walls and floors were smeared with food, crushed sandwiches, bits of salad, fruits, and vegetables. When the studio people saw it, they tripped. They said we had to clean it up and pay for the damages. Instead of cleaning it right away, though, we decided that we would have a water slide contest in the hallway. We took off our shoes and ran and slid as far as we could, some of us falling and busting our butts. Finally we became tired from all the laughing and running. We cleaned up the studio, washed the walls, shampooed the carpet, and went home.

Those were the days I had fun. Those were also the days when we were a little more naïve. It was also before I understood the value of time in the music industry. Time is money, so now we record and go home. Playtime is later.

Everything was new to us then; the excitement we felt in that studio was because this was all a dream come true. As for me, I always knew that I was going to arrive there someday, somehow. Music was in my blood, and my family was musically inclined. When she was fourteen, Mom joined the Martinelles with my dad. It was a white band that did teen hops and they needed singers. By the time she was fifteen, they put their first songs on wax: "Baby Think It Over" was Dad's; "I Don't Care No More" was Mom's song. The record actually hit the charts and they did a little touring. But they didn't make any money off it. The creep who made the deal with them took the money and left. Still, it's a great record, and I burned it into CDs as a gift for my mom. After my parents married, Mom stopped performing, though Dad continued.

We grew up in church, too, where Mom's singing would work the worshippers up into a frenzy. And our holidays are all about singing and eating.

With singing being second nature, I also had big dreams. I'm the type of child who came out headstrong, so I always went for what I wanted—though I wouldn't do anything bad to get it. I would watch television and could picture myself dancing and singing there. I was also cocky. I wasn't nervous about auditioning for anybody. Now I'm a little more aware: I'm scared whenever a new album comes out, thinking, "Oh my God, do you think we'll sell? I hope people like this." I'm a little more critical now. But back then you couldn't tell me I was the jam. I was the J-A-M. I was like, "I'm about to do this. What do you want me to do?"

I didn't care whether I was on my own or with a group. I just wanted to be a star. When I met the producer Jermaine Dupri, I told my mom I felt like I was getting close. My boyfriend didn't believe me, which was really supportive of him. I said, "You don't have to believe me, but I am about to blow up." Then I met Pebbles and a month later I was telling my boyfriend, "I told you so." We thought TLC was going to be the thing, not huge like Michael Jackson or Madonna. No, we wanted to be as big as BBD, the three boys from New Edition who had formed a new group. They were so different and we thought they were just the ultimate. That was before we got the bigger picture.

But I'm getting ahead of myself. In the beginning . . .

Lisa had moved from Philadelphia to Atlanta to be with a different girl group. Things fell through, though, and by coincidence she met Rico Wade, the guy I used to work with at the beauty supply store who gave me my first pair of baggy pants. Rico knew a guy named Ian Burke who had started a lot of groups in Atlanta, and he told him about Lisa and me. At the time, Ian was managing a girl named Crystal who wanted to start a girl group. I was working at the salon and couldn't go to the audition, so I sent a girlfriend of mine in my place. They picked Lisa, but not the friend. Then they said they wanted to come over my house to audition me. That went well, and we became a group called Second Nature.

Ian then introduced us to Jermaine Dupri, a big-time producer who has worked with artists like Mariah Carey and Xscape; he has touched a lot of things. Jermaine wanted us to make a demo so he could try to get us signed. He said I sounded scruffy and that I should sing deep, the bass, and make that my thing. With him we made a demo called "I Got It Going On."

Kevyn Aucoin and me on the set of "Touch Myself" video.

I remembered that Marie Davis, who I used to work with at a salon and who's now TLC's hair designer, once told me that Pebbles was looking for a girl group. About a year and a half had passed since I'd last seen Marie, so I went to visit her. She used to always tell me, "T-T, you going to be a star," so it was funny to think she might help me become one. Anyway, I asked if Pebbles was still looking for a girl group and sure enough she was. I told Marie we didn't have pictures or anything like that, but we were called Second Nature, and we were cool. Maybe Pebbles would want to check us out?

That night Pebbles and Marie called me on a three-way conference call. The next day, Pebbles took Crystal, Lisa, and me out for a meal. The day after that we auditioned, and she said she wanted us to be her girl group. She had a name change for us, too: TLC, for Tionne, Lisa, and Crystal. We were cool with that.

It looked like we were on the verge of signing with Pebbles, but then one day she took Lisa and me aside and said, "I don't think I want a group that has one lacking member. That one member can make the other two look bad." Lisa and I got the point.

When we had auditioned for Pebbles, she asked us each to sing

TLC on the "No Scrubs" shoot.

something. I sang Ice Cube's rap like it was mine. I was thinking, "Hey, I'm about to get me a record deal!" Then Lisa sang and rapped too. When it was Crystal's turn, she said she didn't know what to sing, that we were rapping too fast. She just seemed flustered. This obviously wasn't going to fly for us, so we decided after thinking it over, we'd have to ask her to leave the band.

This wasn't a conversation we wanted to have, but we were so close, and we didn't want anything to jeopardize our chances. This could be our only shot. We went over to Crystal's house with a girl named Josh who worked for Pebbles. I'll never forget what Lisa said: "Girl, we got some good news and some bad news. The good news is Pebbles wants to sign us, but the bad news is, girl, we don't want you in our group no more." I busted out laughing. I just could not believe she said that. Crystal handled it really well. She wished us luck and then asked us to leave. Once we were outside on the porch, Lisa and I

both said, "Damn, that was easier than we thought." I felt bad for her, but I was also relieved. Now we could find another C and get it right.

We put on auditions to find a replacement, but had no luck. LA Reid finally called one day and talked about a girl named Rozonda, whom he had seen audition for something else. We met Rozonda that night and we really liked her. We christened her Chilli. We put a routine together in Pebbles's office, went to her house, and auditioned for Dallas Austin, Kayo, and Darryl Simmons. The co-owners of LaFace records, LA Reid and Babyface Edmonds—in my opinion, the number one songwriter in the world—were also there. When that man tells you a song is going to be a hit, you better believe him. Back then, LaFace was not the force it is today. TLC would become the first artist on that label to break out. We helped build the company before they got big with Toni Braxton and others. Anyway, LaFace offered us a contract. Just like that! We didn't have time to celebrate, though.

Time for the studio.

When LA and Pebbles asked if there was anyone we wanted to work with, I said Dallas right off the bat. He was a new, up-and-coming, hot kid back then. I've known Dallas since I was fifteen, when we used to hang out at Jellybeans. He's not only a good food fighter but he's also a talented producer. He just knows me. In a studio session, he could write everything I'm thinking without my ever saying anything. In fact, Dallas did a lot to convert my poem "Unpretty" into a song. He's the only producer who truly understands TLC, and he has been the main producer on all our albums. He's our man.

We worked up the tracks and every song we did went on the album. Usually you do more songs than you need, so you can pick the best ones. But there didn't seem to be any time for that. We did just enough and put out *Oooooooohhh! On The TLC Tip*. We didn't have that much time to rehearse our performances, but Pebbles put us out on the Hammer tour.

On top of this, we heard our music on the radio for the first time. Lisa, Rozonda, and I were driving around when out of nowhere on the radio comes "Ain't 2 Proud 2 Beg." We couldn't believe it. We pulled into a Taco Bell parking lot, jumped out, and started hooting and hollering and dancing. People in that parking lot thought we had lost our minds, but we didn't care. We made it!

With each album we produced, I seemed to grow a little. I was going through the baggy clothes stage on the first album. On the second, I felt a little sexier. On the third, I felt like an adult, and we went for a more techno look with spacy sounds because of the millennium. The key to TLC's music is that three different individuals, the sound, and our images are as big as our names. And our songs are pretty simple: We talk about life situations that everyone can relate to, add a funky beat and some good music. Each song we do reveals another facet of each or all of us in TLC. Someone once made a comment to me about *Fanmail*, that "Unpretty" didn't sound like TLC. I said, "How can you say 'Unpretty' doesn't sound like me when you don't know all of me? You only know what I gave you on the last two albums. 'Unpretty' is me because I wrote it, and it's TLC's because we embraced it and performed it as a group. If you don't like it, that's another thing, but don't tell me who I am. You can accept me or not. That's your problem."

My career has allowed me to travel all over the world and meet a lot of people I admire, like my favorite singer, Patti LaBelle, as well as Michael Jackson, Janet Jackson, and Prince. Mom is thrilled for me. As long as I don't do anything to disrespect my person, my mom has always supported me. I share all my success and accomplishments with her. I couldn't have done any of this without her. And I've been blessed with great fans. It's satisfying to know that I can make someone's day with my music, something I do from my heart; to know that I reach people in a positive way; to know that I'm making a difference. The confidence from achieving this has led me to aim for more, and it's given me the opportunity to pursue other things: acting, cartoons, and even writing this book.

I appeared in *Belly*, Hype Williams's first movie, and had a lot of fun. Frank Vincent, who's played in mob movies with actors like DeNiro and Pesci, coached me on *Belly*. Frank was a great coach, helping me through the scenes, and he was nice enough to tell people on the set that I could be a star if I wanted to. We'll see.

I've done some other little parts, too, like with TLC in *House Party 3*, and I was in *Living Single*, with TLC and solo. Funny thing is, I love and adore movies but I never thought about acting until people started sending me scripts. In the meantime, I've read for a couple of parts that I actually won over some major players, but because of my obligations to TLC I had to pass. Still, that helped me in the confidence department, and I think there'll be time for acting later.

I would also like to do some work behind the camera. In fact, my producer, Dallas Austin, and I have a movie called *Jellybeans* that we just sold. On the television side, I have a cartoon, *It's a Fly World*, that I'm developing with the Jim Henson Company. And I have a calendar of myself for the year 2000 that's going to be available in stores. I have other dreams, too, but these should keep me busy for a while.

Jellybeans

Dancers of "Creep" video.

A nother great thing about TLC is that it's allowed me to pursue my passion for dancing, which began when I was a teenager, at a place called Jellybeans. It was a roller-skating rink and dance club in Atlanta that helped transform my life. I'd say it got me off the streets. Between Sundays I'd get my outfit together and I'd practice dancing almost every day to prepare to battle people on the dance floor. Creative forces took over, so I stopped fighting and all that stuff. The creativity was a good way to channel my energy, and the fighting and nonsense I used to be involved in disappeared. You may not know this, but Atlanta is known for its unique dance styles that are almost always trend-setting and ahead of their time. And Jellybeans was the place to be on Sundays. When my mom wanted to punish me, all she had to say was that I couldn't go to Jellybeans. I'd break down and have a fit. It was all I had to look forward to; it had become my world. The dancing, the fashion statements, the whole experience was new to me, and by nineteen I was hooked.

Over time I found that I didn't like dancing like a girl. I prefer cool, smooth moves, in pocket and really hard. Girl dancing is too cutesy for me and it just doesn't suit my type. I created a lot of dances for the first two albums, and then on the second one we also started with my boy Deyvne, Derek Stevens, one of the biggest choreographers out today, who works with stars like Puffy Combs and Monica. Deyvne was in a group called FDC, and they created dancing styles for Atlanta. They were like Parliament: people before their time.

I still work up some touches in the dances, and almost every time, I realize that the stuff I learned on the dance floor in Jellybeans still surprises people today. There'll be something I picked up when I was fourteen that'll be new and hot to the world. In "No Scrubs" I made up a dance where I'm moving my hips and hands, which many people complimented me on. Then there are the dances that I created for "What About Your Friend" and "Creep." When I see people doing them on MTV, I know that I'm doing something right.

I think the success of my dancing, and why it's such a big part of TLC, is the attitude behind it. Doing a move or a step doesn't mean anything unless you put some style and energy into it, like you own it. Dancing without attitude is like living without breathing. It just doesn't make sense.

Paul Starr doing my makeup for "Creep," 1995.

There's No Business Like Show Business. At Least I Hope Not.

I fight to survive every day of my life. I've been through a lot of hard days in the music business. I've wanted to throw in the towel on plenty of occasions. I've been depressed, mad, hysterical; I've cried, and I've even made myself ill. I couldn't get over the fact that I was dependent and subservient to a company, all because I signed my name on a contract at the tender age of nineteen. Little did I know I was basically going to become a slave—I'm not exaggerating.

I work hard. We spend hours on end in a studio getting the tracks down, shoot videos at all hours over two or three solid days, and that's just getting started. I dance five to eight hours a day to practice for the tour; then we go out on tour for months at a time. On my days off I do interviews, attend events, and handle business. Now by itself, I didn't mind doing the work, even though the stress did send me to the hospital seven times in one year, almost dying a couple times. The problem was that TLC was generating all this money and Lisa, Rozonda, and I rarely saw any of it. That hurt. It's not fun when you bust your behind and you see someone else profit from it, and you know it's yours. It was hard to find the strength to stick with it. It just blew my mind not having any money while knowing that I was selling millions of records. No one cares if you're starving in this business. You look at some record company's assistant who has a house and drives a Mercedes, and you know my family and I are sitting there, the lights are off, the phone's disconnected. My mom couldn't work because of the herniated disks in her back, and we were barely getting by with her disability checks. It was up to me to provide the income. Meanwhile, somebody's assistant who just takes messages lives better than I do? Where's the fairness in that?

Then you try and go up against all these high-powered people who have been around way longer than you and are way richer than you, and all that does is generate more bills and debts. Then you do things that you wouldn't ordinarily do. I have made some hasty, messed-up decisions I probably wouldn't have made if I had the money. I never did anything I was ashamed of, but there were a couple of jobs and songs that I wouldn't have agreed to if I hadn't needed the money. But I had to look after my mom and brother and pay our bills.

You might be sitting there thinking, child, why did you sign such a foolish contract? I feel we were taken advantage of when we signed. We had one of the top lawyers in the business who told us the contract was fair. I believe he thought we were a fly-by-night group that would just come and go like so many other acts. Maybe the terms didn't matter, because we'd make an album, it would fail, and it would all be irrelevant. Who knows what he was thinking?

During the success of *crazysexycool*, I would be on TV, win awards, sell fourteen million albums and . . . I was bankrupt. How about that? After some ugliness and a lawsuit, we now have the deal we should have had in 1994.

Another strange twist to all of this was that Pebbles was our manager and she was married to LA who not only was co-owner of LaFace, but also co-owner of Pebbletone (for Pebbles and Antonio), which we didn't know at the time. This was a unique situation and obviously it created some conflicts. By the time the mess was over we bought our name, TLC, back from Pebbles. Because she made up the name she owned it. We went through some bad times, but in the end, Pebbles contributed a lot to TLC and I believe she was good in her own way.

I went through the whole period being very bitter, angry with everybody, not liking anything, snapping at people in public. I was hurting myself, making myself sick and delirious. It took a lot for me to be a bigger person and smile at some of the people I smile at. Mom always taught me that you reap what you sow. I don't see how any of those people sleep at night, but things like that have to come back on them. It helped me to see people for who and what they are, and to accept them for it. Now that I can see you, you can't hurt me, and it has helped me become stronger. But that was a big hump to get over.

Here I am, ten years later, in a slightly better situation, but still not free to do exactly what I really want. I try to make the best of it. I'm not bitter anymore. I just get upset sometimes when I ask to do something that brings in money for me, and I am told no, because I signed on the dotted line. The record company has that power over me. I try and look at it like this: there's always something you don't like in every job.

How about going solo and starting over, you might ask. Other people made me think about a solo career. I don't know how many times I've been offered solo deals since I've been with TLC. But I have to go on my feelings. I have sense enough to know that I'm not going to do a solo album just because Mr. Record Executive thinks I should do one. He's thinking about his pockets and not my life. I'm a dollar sign to him. It may not be time for me to go solo. When I'm ready, I will, but I don't necessarily know if I want to do it.

So when kids ask me about the business, all I can think is, "You poor child, you have no idea." The best way to take advantage of this business is to start your own label, put yourself on that label, and make all the money as the artist and the record company and be happy. You make all your own rules. Mack 10's HooBangin' Records, Master P's No Limit Records, Puff Daddy's Bad Boy, Jay-Z's Rockefeller Records: I give these guys big props because they are the CEOs of their own companies. They took control of their business and did not let the business control them. But I didn't have the money to start up my own label, nor do I have the patience.

When you're a new artist, you have very little leverage with a record company. It's like owning a mansion in the middle of the ghetto: You had better watch your back or you'll get robbed. All the 'hood will want to come break in and take all your good stuff. Lawyers, accountants, agents, managers, record company executives. But you can't just say no to business. You must watch your back, and pray to God that you get a good lawyer and he knows what he's talking about.

Outside the money thing, you also need to stay grounded. Never lose sight of who you are and where you come from. With life in general, you need a good base in order to succeed and keep yourself intact—it's no different in the entertainment business. I'm still my mother's child, still the person she raised. Same amount of sassiness, feistiness, attitude. Nothing's changed except for the material things and my growth as a person.

My growth has also meant that I feel more responsible. Especially because I definitely believe that kids are influenced by the music they listen to. Parents should listen and watch what their kids are doing, because with no direction, kids will follow anything. Young people are looking for answers, looking for something to hold on to, to help them define themselves. If they don't have strong role models at home, they'll be looking at the television or listening to the radio for that wisdom. I try to be sensitive to that, and I wish every celebrity would realize he has followers—that he's in a position to help mold and influence young people. Everyone's looking for something to believe in, and I hope they want to make it positive. But if you're getting people to believe in killing chickens; or if you're walking around with your butt hanging out, wearing titties as a man, with red demon eyes and hair like a girl—you're exposing kids to some weird stuff.

Garfield and me at the "Red Light Special" video shoot, 1995.

You can find this stuff too easily on television, as if it's normal and not harmful—but it is. It should be on late at night so adults can choose to watch it if they want to. But kids don't know any better, and before you know it, they'll be emulating someone who might mess up their lives rather than enrich them.

Some performers sing about what they went through, telling stories of the 'hood or their own experiences, which I think is fine. And if Marilyn Manson really thinks worshipping the devil is cool, that's his problem. It becomes everyone's problem, though, if there are kids out there who really buy that message. It's wrong to glorify the violence, to encourage other people to go out and do something harmful. Sharing your experiences, showing people how to overcome, being positive, that's being responsible for your art.

Those material things brought on by money and success can change people, magnifying what was already there. You can't bring something out of me that's not in my spirit or my soul. It just shows who you really are—it either brings out the best in you or the worst in you. With me, sometimes I feel like I didn't change, but the people around me did, everybody looking at me differently because I've been on MTV. What's the difference if I'm a little more popular than the next person? I'm just Tionne all day long.

Nine times out of ten, you get women who are already whores before they got into this business, and that's what they'll do, whore some more. That's the truth about those women. And men, they flaunt—they buy cars and jewelry, they hang with all these boys who are just like them, and leech off them and act like they were the performers. I've always believed a big entourage gives these guys a sense of security and empowerment. With their followers yessing them to death and kissing their butts, they feel like the man.

I think it's safe to say men go broke before women do in this business. There may be some women that are more promiscuous than men, but we hold on to our money. Or the money from the sucka who gave into groupism.

A business is only as good as the people who run it. If my experience in this industry tells me anything, it's that there are a lot of mean, evil, and greedy people running around trying to exploit the artists and entertainers who are just looking for a way to get their message and their art out there. There's hope, though. Just keep your eyes open, keep your faith in God, and surround yourself with people who truly care about you.

Waiting for Daddy

The most powerful memory of my father is the most painful one. It was Christmas Eve and my father had called to say that he would be visiting. "Hey, T-Booger," he said, "I'm gonna come and bring you an Xmas gift. So sit by the window and wait for your daddy to come." It was going to be like the year before, when he came with a present and made me feel special. In our house at 2030 High Street, the living room looked out over the driveway so you could see people as they drove up. I waited by that window. Every once in a while, as it got later and later, my mom would come to me and say, "Let's go to bed, it's getting late." But I kicked and screamed, "No, Daddy's coming!"

Well, I fell asleep on the couch. Come morning time, Auntie Ressie woke me up and said Santa Claus had come. Dad hadn't yet come, but I thought he would still show up. I'll never forget running out in the morning when a car pulled up in front of the house, thinking it was him. When my aunt and uncle stepped out of that car I started shaking and trembling. The reality hit me then that he wasn't going to be coming after all. I was so crushed and disappointed. That Christmas it didn't matter how many gifts I got. Surrounded by the love of the rest of my family, all I could focus on was how I thought my daddy didn't love me.

What made it worse was that he was going to marry his second wife, Cynthia, a week later, on New Year's Eve—which I only found out five years later. He knew he wasn't going to be visiting me, yet he still lied and gave me hope. Why would you tell your little girl that? I should've known, though. The man rarely followed through on his promises.

I do have nice memories of Dad when he used to live with us. He would take me to Smitty's Donuts, and he would never tell me no. He gave me anything I wanted, and he never spanked me. But, to be honest, there aren't that many of those nice memories, and no clear incident that makes me feel like I had a daddy in my life.

Mom says that I used to look just like my dad when I was a baby. I have my father's broad shoulders and I'm shaped like him. I also got my bags and circles under my eyes from both of them. My mom also says I have my dad's temper, stubbornness, and attitude, his "crazy side," but I think Mom's got a lot of that, too. She says I walk like Dad's Native American mother, Annie Watkins.

He was really handsome when he was young. He's medium height, light brown; he also has thick veins in his arms—I always used to push them and play with them when I was young because they were so thick and big. He wore a short Afro and he was always immaculately clean. Mom said he was vain because he would always look in the mirror. I remember he used to brush his mustache in the rearview mirror while he drove.

Dad used to be an inspector with NASA, checking rocket boosters on the space shuttle, which was a good job. Not that he would send any of his money to our house. My mother never saw a dime from him, no matter how badly things were going for us. Today he's a minister and works in a school with underprivileged children. Dad says he's grown and learned a lot through God, that he's a better man now.

My dad left my mom and me when I was three years old. He was a talented singer and trumpet player and was pursuing his musical career in Florida when my parents separated. Mom never remarried. Instead she focused on me, and later, Koko. She didn't have a lot of time for other men.

Dad, on the other hand, was a different story. He married Cynthia when I was seven years old. In fact, Dad, who's three years older than my mom, also married for a third time—to a woman who's three years older than me.

Anyway, when I was a teenager I decided I wanted to spend summers with him in Orlando, Florida. Mom thought I was crazy, but I really wanted to go, to spend time with him. I guess I still loved him despite the hard times. But summers were not fun. Yes, he would take me out shopping or something, but his wives or girlfriends were always messing things up.

I guess his women felt like I was in the way, because some used to do things to me that were just plain wrong. If I was holding his hand, one would move mine aside to take his hand instead. Or she would knock stuff on the floor and tell me to pick it up or else she'd tell my father I did this or that. Or braid my hair so tight that I would get sores on my head. One woman actually told me, "He'll believe me before he believes you." And she was right.

When I went to complain to him, he wouldn't believe me. I felt like my dad wasn't sticking up for me, letting some woman abuse his child, like he loved her but didn't love me. I couldn't understand why you wouldn't stick up for your flesh and blood. If I were my dad, I would've punched her in the face. That's your little girl! I felt that, for him, other women have always been the priority. He's very selfish that way. After two horrible summers, Mom wouldn't let me go back there.

Thing is, I didn't want money or material things from my father, though my mom could have used the help. No, if there was one thing I wanted from him as my father, it was that he not make me feel unwanted or unloved.

It was difficult for my mom to make me understand that my father loved me in his own way, that people make mistakes, that you have to accept them for who they are. I thought, he doesn't love me. Why would he lie or want to be with a girlfriend more than with his own daughter? How could he love me and be so cruel? I never did anything to him. I became mad at the world, bad tempered, rebellious. I had problems at school. I went through hell and lots of tears. Mom sent me to a psychiatrist and I tried not to hear her; I thought, I'm not crazy. I don't understand what I did to him. Why won't he like me? What did I do? Is it my fault?

Dad tried to apologize to me once when I was twenty-five, but by then I was like, "Whatever. It's good that you noticed that you messed up, but it took you how many years to say something to me?" He missed my whole life.

Eventually, though, I had to forgive him. I realized I had so many emotional issues with our relationship that it was messing up my life. I had to accept him for what he was. People are going to be as they are, and there's no need anymore for me to kill myself over it. You can't change people. I understand now that not everyone is meant to be a parent. People make mistakes, and can't take them back, and we can't undo time, but we can make up time. I'm not going to lie about what he's done or how I felt, because it's a part of my life, and it's the truth. But I'm not bitter about it and I don't harp on it anymore. It's a lifetime process, and I dedicate a lot of time to it. I have made it for twenty-nine years without my father in our house, but it helps to know he does love me.

Today Dad has two sons with his new wife. God bless him. I'm glad he can give his two sons what he never gave me and he can get out of them what he missed with me. Because growing up without my father made me realize how important the role of a father is. It's not just being the man who has the ability to make children. It's more than just being a provider. It's about spending time with them, and loving them unconditionally.

For myself, I know I will work hard to make sure I'm the best parent I can be, and if I can help it, I will have the best father for my children. I've gained determination to try and make the best of my life when I get married and have kids.

Unpretty

Up until a couple of months ago I had a problem with my weight. Some people might see it as ridiculous, but to me it wasn't.

I'm very petite, and as a teenager I was really frail. All of my friends were always busty and more developed than me, or at least they seemed so to me at the time. I was always teased a lot for being too skinny, and it gave me a complex. I always felt that guys wouldn't like me because I looked so young.

In the song "Doin' the Butt" a part of the song goes, "Trina gotta big ol' butt, oh yeah, so-and-so has a big ol' butt." All the kids would dance at the parties and chant their names on that part in the song, but when it got around to me they would say, "Tionne ain't got no butt, oh yeah."

Boy, did that hurt my feelings. I started wearing two pairs of pants, one pair of pants up under the other, hoping it made me look thicker. Even if it was hot outside I'd still walk around with these layers on. I carried that complex for a while even after my butt had grown.

Then my complex moved to my legs. I still have the same shape to my legs that I had when I was young. When my friends and I would walk side by side, guys would yell to them, "Damn, your legs are fine." When it came to me, they would only say, "Aw, her legs are so cute." As if I was her little sister, when I was the oldest!

I can look back on those days and laugh now. Thank God! It was so depressing back then. Even if I got a compliment, if a blemish appeared on my face, I couldn't believe it. I thought it was abnormal. Every now and then I still have a complex here and there, especially about the dark circles and bags under my eyes that appear when I'm tired or ill. But what can you do? Despite what you see in magazines, music videos, movies, or television, no one is flawless or perfect. There is a lot of makeup, air brushing, shrinking, stretching, thinning—you name it, it can be done, especially now with powerful computers. And I only know this because I'm there seeing all the things they can do to entertainers' images before, during, and after a photo or video shoot.

Society and media make us feel insecure about ourselves. Just look at our culture of celebrity worship. It's all about celebrities' breasts, butts, abs, their clothing, and how they wear their hair. Some of these are genuinely beautiful girls. They're natural and don't require a lot to look good. But I'm telling you there are some real makeup queens who are worked on by a stylist and a makeup artist for a couple hours before they appear in public. It's just not realistic to measure ourselves against these people.

This might seem like a digression, but one of the reasons I love *The Sopranos* on HBO (do not call my house on a Wednesday night— *Oz* and *Sex in the City* are my other favorite shows) is that all the characters look realistic. They're all complicated people dealing with big life issues. (The main character happens to be a mob boss, but that's beside the point.) And they look like your neighbors, the people you see walking down the street, at the store, or on the subway. These aren't the perfect people you usually find on television. Soap operas and other beautiful-people shows have their place, but it is cool to see a show where real people struggle. Who couldn't connect with that?

I was so happy to see Camryn Manheim (from *The Practice*) win an Emmy and take up the cause for overweight women. She's done a lot for herself, succeeding in a business that is not kind to big women. I know a lot of beautiful big women, but they still have their challenges. Most women still feel they need to be skinny to get a man and be sexy, which I understand. But if a man doesn't love you for who you are, he ain't worth having around. If he's that immature to be caught up by the size of a woman's breasts or her butt or whatever, then he's just a plain old scrub. Real men can see right into a woman's heart and soul and embrace them for it.

Not that I've met many extraordinary men. I modeled myself after my mom, a strong, independent woman who can do for herself. Most guys feel intimidated meeting a woman like that, so I need a man who's secure with himself. It's also tough for a guy to be with a woman who earns more money and is perceived to be more successful. They feel less of a man. It'll come out in an argument where he'll say something like, "You're saying that because you look down on me for not doing as much as you do." If a man's comfortable with what he's about, he shouldn't be thinking things like that.

I guess it would be easier to be with a guy who was equally successful or more successful than I was. If not, that's okay, but I don't need a scrub. If he's someone who is trying to do something for himself, I'll help him get on his feet, but I'll be damned if I'm working and he's sitting on his butt. That is just not going to happen.

Whoever God puts in front of me to be my husband, he's going to be strong, honest, outgoing, spunky, and have a sense of humor. He should be smart, not necessarily academically smart, but with common sense and street sense. He's also got to be honest and communicative. I don't want to go through what my mom experienced with my dad.

I also hope he looks good. I have a thing for guys with gold or caramel-colored skin. Antonio Sabato, Jr., is about as white as it would get for me. I've only had three boyfriends my whole life—one was light-skinned and two were brown, and I don't understand that. How'd it happen? Just goes to show you how unpredictable life can be. Still, I was raised in a family where color didn't mean anything, so I'll keep my options open.

I don't really date though. If you took me on a date, you'd have to take me and all my girls out. A guy might like me but I'm not sure, so I say, "You'll have to take me, Nechole, TaeTae, or Julie out or I'm not going." Most guys agree to do it. I've seen cute guys and don't feel a connection, so I'll try to set him up with my friend. I don't easily develop a relationship with a man because I don't like strange people touching me. I was with my first boyfriend for seven and a half years, dated two other guys, and it's been two years since I broke up with the last one. I think I'm about to have a fourth, but we'll see what happens.

The first time I was lovesick I felt like hell. I was sad, moping around the house, not doing much of anything. Mom told me to get off my butt. "That boy ain't thinking about you," she'd say. "Occupy your time, do something. Be productive and soon you won't be thinking about him anymore." That was good advice.

My own advice would be to put your mind before your heart. Don't put anything past anybody. Love with your eyes open, and don't be foolish enough to ignore any problems. Make sure your partner respects you, and if he's not doing you right, dump him. The pain you feel will go away a lot faster than the pain of being in a miserable relationship that should've ended a long time ago.

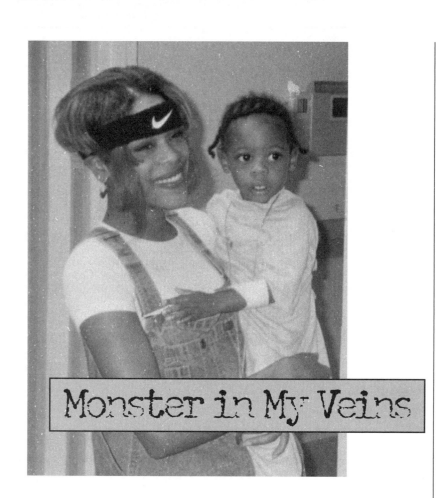

Monster in My Veins

Many doctors have told me that my career is killing me, and my mom agrees with them. She constantly worries that the stress of performing, being on the road, and keeping up with an intense schedule will one day do me in. But I can't think about that. God put me on this earth to use my talents, and until the day I find I have another art that I can pursue with the same passion, I'm going to keep on doing what I'm doing. So I ask doctors to tell me how to survive and maintain my career. After all, I want to live, not die. Killing myself won't help anyone, but I need to live on my own terms.

In sickle cell anemia, the red blood count is abnormally low, so that oxygen doesn't flow properly through the bloodstream to the lungs. It causes cells to sickle, or to clot in the joints. The pain can be excruciating because your blood is not moving. When I was a newborn, I used to cry a lot, but my mom had no idea why. After running a series of tests, they finally diagnosed me with sickle cell anemia and allegelic arthritis. When I was twenty-eight, I finally found out exactly what I have: 83 percent sickle cell traits mixed with a percentage of arthritis and betathalacimia. But there wasn't much they could do about it.

By the time I was seven I had gone through a lot of crises, and to this day they still haunt me. Sometimes with the doctor's help, and most of the time through trial and error with my mom, we figured out what would cause a crisis: too much heat, drinking milk, colds, swimming in a cold pool or the ocean, playing in snow, handling anything cold out of the freezer, being punched, stress, exhaustion. Just about everything has made me sick. When I was younger I didn't want to admit I had it, so I went against the rules, and that really messed me up. I felt I didn't have to accept that something was wrong with me, that I could ignore it and I'd be fine. I wanted to be normal and to do what everyone else was doing. I'm not like that anymore, though. These days I'm careful to avoid doing things that cause crises, which are real doozies.

I start aching, sometimes in really excruciating pain. When it's really bad, it's as if someone is stabbing me with a butcher knife over and over wherever it hurts. The only parts of my body that have never hurt are my feet and my fingers. I've had pain everywhere else at one time or another. It can affect my whole body, or sometimes it can be just a leg. If it's my legs, I can't walk and I have to learn how to walk again. If it's my arms, I can't hold anything, so people have to help feed me. I feel painful and weak. I've been in so much pain that I get delirious, not knowing where I'm at. Or my face might swell up to a point where you wouldn't recognize me.

Whenever we suspected a crisis coming on, my mom would take me to the doctor. Nine times out of ten, he'd say I have to be admitted. We'd go home, pack my suitcase, stop and get me a special treat. She'd take me to Mustard's for some sugar biscuits or to Tasty Tacos, anything that would make me stop crying. I'd be happy for a little bit, then cry again, saying, "I don't want to go back there!"

When I was a child, my mom would take me to the toilet and sit me down to do my business. But I didn't want any of that. No matter what the pain, I would crawl to the bathroom before I had to ask her anymore. Even if it took me thirty minutes and I cried all the way there, I was going on my own. When I'm in the hospital, it'll hurt, but I'll tell the nurses to leave me be, that I'm going to walk alone. There are times I'll have them help me get there, but then they've just got to leave me to myself. They'll knock on the door to see if I need help and I'll say, "I'm fine. Just a little drugged up. I'm going to sit here for about an hour."

Most of the doctors and nurses I've dealt with have been terrific people, but there are some that need better bedside manners. Good doctors care about the person in total; they don't just see them as a patient but a human being. Ask me how I'm doing. I've got a name. Good nurses show they care. Others don't even look at you. Once my mom left the room to go to the lobby for ten minutes. I wasn't feeling well and did not want to eat anything. So this nurse is standing there with a spoonful of liver and I'm telling her, no, thank you. Well, she forced my mouth open and smashed the liver down my throat. That woman got a nice beat down from my mom when she got back, and lost her job.

I don't know what I'd do without my mom. I remember there was a kid in the hospital with Down's syndrome who would not stop crying. The nurses wouldn't pay any attention to her and the doctors would just probe her and go away. The baby never had a visitor. One day she was really crying and I managed to walk over and sit next to her crib. I reached through the bars and I held her hand. She stopped crying. That's all she needed: just a sign that somebody cared.

My mother never left me alone. Even today, if I'm in the hospital and she has an emergency to tend to, a cousin or friend will stand by. Nothing's ever going to happen to me without someone seeing it. It makes me feel better just knowing that. The best medicine is to find my mom at my bedside smiling at me when I wake up. For twenty-nine years, she has always been there for me. I have a song I put on my audiobook that she would sing to comfort me when I was a baby: "I have a girl, a pretty little girl, her name is Tionne-Tenese? Oh Tionne, Tionne-Tenese?"

In the hospital, I have to drink lots of fluids and get hooked up to an IV to flush the blood. I also get hooked up to oxygen until the blood recovers. Meanwhile, my body fights against itself because the doctors prescribe drugs that constipate, then they give me other drugs that act as laxatives. They're also drugging me up to cover the pain. And these are some powerful painkillers. You go into the hospital with one problem and leave with another. Now you feel like a crackhead or a heroin addict. I'm allergic to morphine, so they use Demerol on me. Recently they tried a new drug that is supposed to be the equivalent of morphine, but my body reacted wrong to it. I threw up, broke out, scratched my skin uncontrollably. That in addition to my usual symptoms, and I was all whacked out. Once I get off the drugs, I go through withdrawal, with hot and cold flashes, shaking and jumping with crazy dreams, and it's hard to breathe. In the meantime, my body is sweating out the drugs so I smell like all these chemicals.

The withdrawals are so traumatic Mom insists I stay at her house each and every time I leave the hospital. She protects me from any craziness going on around me and just lets me focus on getting better, getting back in touch with myself and my body. She always makes the best of it, and I sometimes feel I have to stay strong not only for me but also for her. My mother taught me the value of strength, not feeling sorry for myself, understanding, and most importantly that she and God love me.

There are still a lot of unanswered questions about sickle cell. There are different versions of the disease, and people are affected in different ways. My cousin, Donnie Buford, for instance, has full-blown sickle cell anemia. He goes to the hospital a lot because of his constant battle with pneumonia. And with him sometimes morphine doesn't even work on the pain, and his fevers run so high, they've they got to put him in a bathtub full of ice.

I think we need more research and to get more aggressive about helping the minorities out there who suffer from this disease. That starts by making people more aware of how horrible and disabling this disease is. Bill Cosby and Sidney Poitier used to speak about sickle cell, and I'm happy to continue on for them.

Because I actually have the disease and am a celebrity, I'm in a position where people listen to me—I can reach people—so I decided to become a spokesperson for the Sickle Cell Foundation. Through the help of various individuals and companies, I've been able to get donations for the foundation, which has meant a lot to me. Being out there, I've discovered that the lack of funding for research into this disease has less to do with the racial thing or people's apathy. It's just that not enough people know about it. There's not enough awareness of a disease that affects a population that isn't always empowered. I'm happy to be bringing attention to it.

We'll have it beaten yet. As for me, I don't intend to let it keep me from doing the things I love to do, that make me who I am. You can call that stubborn, but I just call it living.

The
Thoughts
Behind
My Poems

"Unpretty"

I think that almost everyone has had the feeling of being unpretty. I know I have, especially after leaving the hospital after a sickle cell crisis. Some people would say that I was looking good, which I couldn't understand. I would feel so ugly on the inside that I would think I was ugly on the outside, too.

Do any of us think we look good enough? Are any of us completely happy with the way we look? Whether it's a man thinking he's too short or skinny, or a woman thinking she's not good enough for her mate because he's staring at someone else or has left her, society has made us think about what being pretty is. Whose standards do we have to stand up to? Society's? Or our own? The first nose job wasn't enough. Neither was the third face-lift, liposuction, or breast implant. Who determines what the perfect person is? No one is flawless. Feeling pretty starts from within.

"Bitter"

I know a lot of bitter people. What they need to do is let those bad feelings out, find someone to talk to. Otherwise your attitude will worsen and you will go around all unhappy and stuff, wasting your time thinking about someone who is probably not thinking of you. Your bitterness isn't going to change them. Don't be afraid to change, get rid of that boyfriend that makes you feel worse, change your job if it's killing your spirit. Surround yourself with positive and uplifting people.

Bitterness wears on your body and makes you get old fast. Why give yourself extra problems when there's an easier solution? Let it go!

"The Mirror"

The mirror is about people who like to steal joy away from others. I used to let people get to me, upset me, and affect my mood, but not anymore. Once you see people for who and what they are, it can't bother you anymore. Accept it and go on being the person you are and never let them get to you. Maybe one day they'll look into the mirror and they'll see their true selves.

"Hatred"

It's just a bad way to live life. You miss out on all the good because you focus on so much that is bad! There has to be a reason for so many people to be filled with hate. Is it us who make you so unhappy that you hate yourself? If you hate, you can't love, and believe me, love's a much better way to live.

"Confused"

Be proud of who you are. If you're hiding or lying about something that you are doing or have done, there's no way that you are really comfortable with it. If you can't admit it, quit it!

"That's a Child"

I just can't imagine why someone would do harm to a child. I can only pray for those who need the help to stop molesting children, and pray for the poor children and hope they can find help. Maybe they will never forget what happened, but a scar can heal. If it happens to you or someone you know, please find a way to tell someone so that bad person can be stopped. You're helping them and most of all helping yourself.

"A Killer"

Being an innocent and helpless victim to crime can cause hateful feelings to build up in one's heart. If someone keeps violating a person who can't fight back, it can cause the victim to want to get rid of that person or thing that hurt her. I think of children who are molested or raped by someone they know, like a family member, and sometimes in their minds the only way to make the pain go away is to get rid of the problem. Who do we blame? Do we blame the child for seeking revenge or the person that caused these feelings to surface?

"Take a Deep Breath"

I take deep breaths when I'm nervous and it really does help. It's not good to keep things bottled up inside. Slowing your breathing down and filling your lungs will help you become more relaxed. It's not a cure, a way to make your problems go away, but it is a way to refresh you and charge up your batteries.

"Special"

My mother is special to me, as is all that she's given me to be able to grow into the woman I am today. If there is anything you have that is special to you, cherish it. Never take things or people for granted. You'll realize how important they were to you when they're gone, when you can't hold them or touch them anymore, and by then it's too late. Appreciate what you have every day.

"The Voice"

This poem may be eerie to some. I believe that some of the people who say they hear voices really do. That's not to say that some are not classified as being sick or crazy, but some are vulnerable and are easily taken over by a darker side. One solution is to find God or something positive to believe in to get rid of all those negative vibes.

"Weight"

A lot of my friends trip about their weight. I did for years (about being too small). Don't put yourself down because of your size. If you're truly unhappy with your body, try to do something about it. But don't sit around and feel sorry for yourself.

"Parenthood"

I know all people are not made to be parents. So sometimes I wonder why they have children in the first place. Being a parent is a very hard job, and your performance as a parent makes a difference in the child's upbringing, outcome, and outlook on life. Raising your child is something that takes a lifetime of dedication. God bless all the parents that do so. I know it isn't easy, but that's life and we all have to do our part.

"Racism"

I think this poem speaks for itself. No two people with the same color of skin are alike.

We're all different but we all bleed the same. End of story.

"You"

This is a poem dedicated to those who never came to see me in the hospital when I was ill, but were supposed to be close to me. I had to learn to get over the feelings of being hurt or neglected. I also had to learn to stop putting others before me, that my health is more important than anything else.

You know who you are. No hard feelings, huh?

"Celebrities"

We work in a backstabbing business that some might kill to succeed in. But no single person is better than another based on what they've done, have, or how popular they are. Society sometimes treats people that way. But ask yourself how humble you are if you are successful. Do you donate to charity because it is something you honestly believe in or because it looks good and is a nice tax write-off? Are you entitled to more because you can act or sing? Does that matter in heaven or hell? I don't think God's going to care how many box office records you've broken or how many hit records you have. We should be remembered for doing good, for helping others, all the while staying humble.

"Get a Job"

If a person has two jobs or does what it takes to get the bills paid, can't you at least get one? Taking the easy way out through a life of crime, illegal businesses, and fast money is no way to live. Work hard to get what you want. When that day comes, when you've accomplished something amazing, you'll feel better about yourself. And you won't be looking over your shoulder anymore.

"Crime"

Crime doesn't pay—at least not in the end.

"The Groupie/Groupism"

To the ladies—one question: How can anyone respect you if you don't respect yourself? And if you don't care about respect, God bless you!

To the fellas—four words: *You are so easy!*

"I Wanna Be Free"

The record industry has a way of making you feel like a slave. Imagine working for your boss and you put in eighty hours. You get paid every Friday, but he doesn't want to pay you your money just because he has the power to withhold your check, or pay you on Wednesday—two weeks from the due date. Or you work eighty hours, but he pays you for working five and a half hours. You have to prove it, but by proving it you'll lose your job or go broke due to the prolonged litigation process. I've felt like I've been blackmailed, with people saying things like, "If you don't work all night, I won't pay you!" I want to sing for the fun of it, not because I'm forced to because of a signature on a piece of paper. I sometimes ask myself, "If the same paper sat in front of me today, would I have signed it?"

"A Sick Life"

I can relate to being in the hospital. I've been hospitalized off and on during the course of my life. I could look at this situation in a lot of different ways, but I choose to look at it in a positive light.

"What's My Name"

A lie is a lie. A little white lie, a bold-faced lie, they are all just vicious things that have hurt so many people. I wrote this poem as if "lie" were a person. "Lie" would be our best friend because that's the first thing we think to do when we're uncomfortable about something or to stay out of trouble. Living a life of lies is a hard way to live. Would telling the truth be easier? Or not doing things we have to lie about?

"Why"

"Why" is a question that is often thought about when certain situations take place. But questioning the unquestionable only confuses me more. So I answer myself by saying all things happen for a reason and some things are just meant to be.

"Wishes"

It feels good to give, to spend time with the less fortunate. There are kids I met through the Make a Wish Foundation that I keep in touch with, and they have really enriched my life. Time is something that doesn't cost anything, so spend a little with people who don't have as much as you. And always try to put yourself in someone else's shoes and try to treat him as you would want to be treated. That's my wish!

"It's Murder"

Abortion is a very touchy subject. I just feel it should be called what it is. The excuse that you're getting rid of nothing, because the child hasn't had a chance to grow, is plain wrong. If the baby were nothing you wouldn't try so hard to get rid of him. He's just in the early stages of life and has a little soul that is getting ready to live.

Abortion should not be used as a method of birth control. While I understand there are those who try to protect themselves and use every form of contraceptive imaginable and still end up pregnant, abortion under those circumstances still doesn't make it right. Just an opinion!

"Not a Punk"

It's unfortunate when children jump in or are forced into gangs. But if you choose to be in a gang, know that there's more to life. Embrace it.

"Late Night Calls"

When the phone rings after midnight and before six A.M., and there's a man inviting you to his place, you should know that there's only one thing on his mind (and it's not sleeping). If you know you don't want the same thing, don't go to say no. That can only lead to something ugly. Think about it.

Tionne's Daily Top 20 List: A Guide for Self-Improvement

1. Love and respect yourself. No one will respect you if you don't respect yourself.

2. Treat people how you want to be treated.

3. No one is perfect or flawless.

4. Try to find something positive to believe in.

5. There's always somebody worse off than you are. (Trust me, there is!)

6. Two wrongs don't make a right.

7. You reap what you sow.

8. Accept people for who they are. Don't let anyone steal your joy.

9. Personal hygiene does matter . . . first impressions last.

10. Everything happens for a reason.

11. If you can get over a death, you can surely get over a breakup with a woman or a man.

12. Appreciate the small things, for some have nothing to appreciate at all.

13. The term "friend" is used too loosely. A "true" friend loves unconditionally. A friend does not:
- sleep or flirt with anyone you are in a relationship with, or your exes;
- talk behind your back;
- take advantage of you;
- accept anything in return when they give of themselves;
- make nationality an issue.

14. To learn, you have to listen; to listen you must hear; and to hear means you have understanding.

15. Always walk into a room with your head up.

16. If you are ashamed of anything you do, then there's something wrong with it. You should be able to be proud of who you are and what you do.

17. It's okay to take chances and to create things unheard of.

18. You can't see if you don't open your eyes—just because you can see the pupils does not mean the eyes are open. Helloooo . . .

19. Be a leader, not a follower.

20. God is good and through Christ all things are possible!

aww, you shouldn't have...

quotes from colleagues

"Tionne's poetry not only reveals her inner self, it sheds light on feelings most of us have. From now on, we will no longer know her as just T-Boz the singer, but Tionne the poet."

—Patti LaBelle, Artist, Entertainer, Author

"She is one of the most sexy and talented young women in the entertainment business today, and her unique style of vocals separates her from any other female in this business."

—Ralph Hawkins, Producer

"As a fan, I anticipate and revel in your music. As a friend, I enjoy your intellect and humor. As a man, I appreciate your sensuality and inner beauty. As a child of God, I am touched by your strength, courage, and spirit. You're all things good created under the sun. You're woman—and nothing compares to you."

—Preston Whitmore II, Writer, Director

"Working with celebrities every day, you start to get a feel for the ones who will be around for a long time. It is apparent to me that Tionne will be in this genre as long as she chooses. She has written a refreshingly honest book from the heart that will give the reader a personal look inside this multidimensional talent's soul."

—Julienne Mijares, Fashion Stylist, Writer, Director

"I just love that breathiness in T's voice. She has a unique sense of style and is a kind person."

—Paula Cole, Artist, Songwriter

"With my being a part of the start of Tionne's career, I feel very proud to see her develop as one of the world's biggest artists, a businesswoman, and now as an author."

—Jermaine Dupri, Artist/Producer, CEO of So So Def Recordings

"I remember when Tionne first began to explore, writing her internal expressions of humanistic pain. She revealed a keen awareness of eclectic emotions in the world. *Thoughts* evokes a passage where street edge meets passion. *Thoughts* is a subtle epiphany, which makes us think about how we treat each other and ourselves. I am so glad my friend decided to share her *Thoughts* with us."

—Salita Gray, Freelance Writer

"Have you heard . . . Tionne is letting us into her soul. With this book, she's giving us a sneak peak into her world. Come in and enjoy her words."

—Jody Gerson, SVP of EMI Publishing

"Tionne is one of the purest people I know. Professionally and personally, her perception comes from the heart and carries a unique quality of its own."

—Dallas Austin, Producer

"T-Boz is one of the most creative artists of our decade. I was totally taken aback by her book, and no doubt it will affect others the same. Her topics are things we take for granted, but should be more aware of. She is truly blessed and gifted. I'm very proud of her."

—Darryl Simmons, CEO of Silent Partner Productions

"Tionne's creativity manifests itself in many different forms. From painting to performing to writing—all of which have unparalleled standards of sincerity."

—Leslie Braithwaite, Producer and Engineer

"When I first met T.T., my first thoughts were on how can I make her my girl. I was captivated by her beauty, talent, and her sex appeal, but that was before I knew how thoughtful, caring, funny, and sometimes stupid she can be. Even though I'm still trying to make her my girl, I wouldn't trade our friendship for anything in the world."

—Ricky Bell of New Edition and Bell Biv Devoe

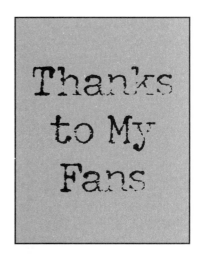

Thanks to My Fans

Ashley Nicole Wilson
Antonio Jackson
Lydia Rose Newman
Peggy Louise Cooper
Raymond Jones
Colleen Nicole Dasch
Elisabeth Diane Buchta
Dionne Jupiter
Kathleen V. Holifield
Aqueelah R. Evans
Semica Gradney
Jessica Bannerman
Lacrayshal Dalton
Tracey Alford
Aric Alford
Miranda Meriam Coffey
Pamela Nichol
Kevondria
Becky Davis
John Walker
Melissa Egan
Natalie McClain
Edna Glover
Louis Glover
Taina Aiisha Comiskey
Jessica Ann Roper
Santana Frasier
Celia J. Barnwell
Calida Motley
Sheena Groves
Katie Lousie Jennings
Faith Lockett

Amanda Deptula
Linda Estep
Dawnstar Bourget
Craig Walker, II
Amber Michelle Rosa
Jamie Rochelle Little
Mina McCall
Cynthia Faith Hilaire
Ivana Simpraga
Ebony Chaunte Fleming
Chansa Tembo
Brittney Nicole Davis
Sarah Mayle
Ronnie DeMarlo Baisley
Terrelle Deas
Jennifer Hamilton
Ki Ki Streeter
Apple B. Lewis
Jasmin Desiree Peita
Ashley Rae Molina
Janise Daleth Zamora
Brittany Alison Clemens
Damien Streeter
Kizzy LaChelle Burgess
Joshuah C. Smith
Eric Beaumont
Eric Blowtorch
Simeon Yianni
Carla Whitaker
Linda Elizabeth Peralte
Shawn Streeter
Jasmine Williams

Jennifer Hanson
Shatel Graves
Tracey Streeter
Krystal Singleton
Rick Streeter
Ashley Messing
Becky Davis
David Lee
Robbie Lee
Jennifer Clark
John L. Barnwell
RL Tucker
Phylicia Danza
Robin Martin
C.E. Dorsey, III
Santana Frasier
Brandon Buie
Lauryn Erickson
Marie-Louise Jersin Nissen
Mike Johnson
Katie Jennings
Detisha Lavohn Council
Jorge B. Contreras, Jr.
Tom Miller
Regina Murray
David Hoffmann
Andrew McDonald
Cynthia Faith Hilaire
Billy Joe Smith
Seretha Johnson
Gemae Williams
Ebony C. Fleming
Jamie Boeckermann
Vanessa McLeod
Alberta Edmonton
Larese Mia Lee
Leah Choi
Amelia Sullivan
Santana Frasier
Cassandra Liddell
Megan Howard
Roderick Evans
Jason Worthy
Michie Quinit
Ralph Williams
Darlene Irvine

Michelle M. Tangi
Myeisha Caesar
Shakaja Wingo
Nelson Duane Hoeppner
Tosha Michelle Mosley
Olga Torres
Andrew Miles
Jamin Champion
Lashawndra Dickerson
Skyler Murchison
Sarah Barna
Kassondra Watson
Joanna Horton
Ashanti Danielle Chamberlain
Serena Shum
Monique LaCole Lyons
Tascha Byrd
Kim Demaddis
Fatima Yousef
Antonia Williams
Laree Banister
Kelly Mae Boggess
Allie Liz Maness
Jamari Akil Douglas
Leandra Espinosa
Amethyst Nike Jones
Hollie Hawkins
Michael Jhon Taylor
Tiphini Lauren Williams
Rowena Garcia Custodio
Caris Harper
Terrell Rolle
Rachel Pollard
Sandra McInnis
Jeff Wagner
Stephanie Wagner
Katy O'Connell
Joseph Lemmons Reddick
Kathleen Nelson
Daryla Quintana-Ruiz
Cedric Quintana
Princene Doe
Jenna Bryant
Michael Harbor
Laura Gibby
Emma Sails

Angela Marie Wright
Lorenzo Murchison
Mike Sayam Burt
Ciara Monique Sutherland
Jasroop Grewal
Lacy McClellan
Michele Terese Redmond
Serena Shum
Rachel McIntyre
Keoni Williams
Linda Taw
Michelle Smith
Melanie Sherrie Sanders
Jayson Percy
Monique Marshall
Ashley Reid
April Garcia
Rachel Cantor
Latoya Leathers
Renee Gillett
Heidi Mullenbach
Jerome Wise
Darilyn May
Sheena Walters
Jamal D. Jolly
Ferdie M. Mider
Julie Ann Hess
Tracie Michelle Contois
Carla Ellis
Decat Annick
Rachel Pollard
Steve Hammer
Kisha Jenkins
Jamila Murchison
Amanda Meso Witkowski
Antika De'Shonna Truitt
Dustin May
Charisse T. Dunn
Sophia Tran
Nikolas Rexhaj
Roger Lloyd
Kareem Grogan
Maleek Murchison
Illi Mai
Misherald Brown
Nicole Marie McQuarrie

Shelly Leigh Kuss
Kasmira E. Hamlet
Kristoff Brass
Thieny Nguyen
Erika Luancing
Kiki Streeter
Ivana Simpraga
Miyako Franklin
Shanel Monier
Michael Thomas Baker
Teri Brady
Shawn Taquan Anderson
Teri Lenoir Brady
Shakaja Wingoo
Kamaria Hadiya Lofton
Casey B. Rooney
Brandon D. Pailin
Tashanda L. Carter
Hayward Aaron IV
Jason Andrew Worthy
Katie Lesosky
Jason Andrew Worthy
Katie Lesosky
Melissa Kathmann
Krystyna Chavez
Chrystelle Santos
Kim-meko Pennie
Maria Connie de la Paz
Fabian Hoen
Danielle J. Williams
Camille Antoinette Hewitt
Tiffany Clayter
Corey S. Gordon
Kristi Grau
Lisa Truong
Kristle Craig
Allison Sawyer
Adam Durand
Tonya Fraser
Kristal Mains
Rachel Cantor
Lisa Maree Kay
Johnathan Brunson
Hyacinth Suarez
Ju'Rae L. Strozier
Renea Monique Brea

Annie Ayanwale
Stephanie Hartzell
Jayson D. Percy
Catherine Bones
Lindsey D. Watkins
Richard Ayar
Sopia Hean
Paul James Mallory
Mercedes TaVon Newton
Damien Streeter
Paige Thomas
Ayisha Bonner
Elizabeth Marcelin
Maurene Indoija Payne
Jill Kincer
Vondra Michelle Calhoun
Pierre-Luc Dusablon
Kelly Lyn Shelton
Tiffany Green
Porsche Rasha Woods
Racquel Reid
Deniz Yurdatap
Alizah Nashira Bright
Michael Liao
Aisha Elston
Mocca Perpetua
Cornelius Daniels
Rabecka Marie Collins
Laura Goble
Kathleen Mei Nelson
Jennifer Shide
Judy Tso
Cedric Quintana
Jon "PJ" Reyes
Lina Salazar Ortegon
Jorge B. Contreras
Ashleigh Madison
Nicole R. Jones
Calicia Nicole Trainor
Aisha Elston
Byron Terell Ross
Renesha A. Daniels
Biyako Franklin
Ashanti Danielle Chamberlain
Sven-Christian Froehlich
Joana Horton

Brandi D. Watkins
Keoni R. Williams
Raquel A. Diaz
Blair Samuel
Shanna Lynn Weeks
Michelle Denise Smith
Cree Walker
Michelle Smith
Tiffanni Gilliard
Candice Marie Fabela
Lancia Draper
Sarah Juanita Preston
KiKi Trice
Generro Walker
Asia Chante' Carroll
Jamal D. Jolly
Nian-Shiang Cheng
Amy Ruth Gersztyn
Montario Briddy
Rachel McIntyre
Shanrika Mercedes Hardeman
Monique York
Fallon Nicole Gill
Uri Smiley
Seurinane Sean Espa Ola
Gaille Chua
Vanette White
Erica Broyals
David Huynh
Kerry Hofferber
Angel Chavez
Crystal Latoya Milton
Maria Rios
Tiffanni Gilliard
Reynaldo B. Ancheta
Shawn Streeter
Gaille Chua
Vanessa Dauterive
Jennifer Lehrer
Ralph Herman Misa
Kristi Kay Grau
Hassan Ali Chouaib
Linh Le
Randy Walker, Jr.
Susan McGregor
Sara Bibby

Tracey Alford
Aric Alford
Dannielle Heron
Amber Rhome
Maurice Jerel Reaves
Laura Anderson
Kimberly Hayes
Tarren Manor
Samantha Sinclair
Edwin Gonzalez
Jennifer Harvey
Brandy Marshall
DJ Malee
Asia Carroll
Hayward Aaron IV
Jacqueline Rodriguez
Chrystelle Santos
Matthew Dans
Evelyn Streeter
John Walker
Rick Streeter
Dionne Jupiter
Raymond Jones
Derek Brooks
Linda Estep
Renee Gillett
Curtis Smith
Shirelle McSwain
Brandi D. Watkins
Tiffanni Gilliard
Jamal D. Jolly
Sheena Walters
Courtney A. Reiff
Keith Tucker
Sarah Zinkann
Stewart Gillespie
Tiffany Ford
Anna Avanesian
Alvin Lawrence Walker
Nerea Domenech
April Gracia
Billie Jo Reeve
Angela Plafcan
Katie O'Gara
Michael Franks
Janna Pankey

Blake N. Vu
Sarah Khan
Esteban Granado
Tiara Blake
Tasha Hendershot
Darcie Newton
Xiao-Mo Yuan
Jamie M. Bender
Kimberly Jackson
Austin Micheal Cash
Ginger R. Jones
Christine Tuttle
Brenda Tireaon Huiel
Andrej Mecava
Tashanda L. Carter
Lancia Draper
Monique Moore
Herbert McLaughlin
Janai Pinkney
Katie Lesosky
Marissa Watkins
Deniz Yurdatap
Lea Espinosa
Niki Jones
Darold L. Ford
Royce Anthony
Stephen Rodrigo
Chrystelle Santos
Gavin Davis
Jamie Nager
Shane Andrew Whatley
Mandy Leann Raines
Janna Drover
Jesse James Williams
Kea Gaynelle Anderson
Nyasha T. Moyana
Cara Yupangco
Princene Doe
Desiree Silva
Verita Adena Carver
Alia S. Al-Hashimi
Jamie Marcotte
Katanya Myers
James Terrell Turner
Ashley-Shayne Nazareno
Janina Guthke

Angela Plafcan
Kate Frankish
Jordan Liberty
Marissa Watkins
Adina Marie Maheux
Danny Thomas
Katie Ann Emmert
Jeremy Reid Chones
Shanna Lynn Weeks
Kimani Fisher
Brittany Street
Emma Sails
Leandra Espinosa
Danny Thomas
Courney R. Collins
Henri Da Cruz
Ann Catherine Johnson
Curtis Smith
Crystal LaToya Milton
Aisha Elston
Joanna Horton
Reynaldo B. Ancheta
Terrell Rolle
Jesse Aaron Landavaso
Janelle Powell
Joseph McKinney
Bhaa Elashkar
Antonio Rontrell Jefferson
Jennifer Barton
Ashley Parisi
Jenna Lynn Bryant
Alexandria Woodruff
Sanchia Jackson
Latonya Walker
Desiree Peel
Princene Doe
Jamie Nager
Danielle Franks
Michie Qunit
Emily Jarvis
Jesse Aaron Landavaso
Coureil Pierre
Katie Butler
Kiana Kelley
Naima Gaskin
Vanessa Yielding

Nicole Kern
Wynne Azevedo
L. Renee Weber
Camilla Robinson
Danielle Samples
Deborah Robinson
Kassondra Watson
Alicia Seamon
Jason Worthy
Donna Booth
Joseph L. Strickland
Peter Kingsley
Michelle Sabrina Peter
Shanrika Hardeman
Angela Plafcan
Brandon Pailin
Camille L. Washington
Shanita M. Moore
Asia Carroll
Yeva Kulidzhanova
Courtney Scott
Denise Voshall
Gabrielle Talley
Ashley Walker
Aly Wingler
Sherrell M. Alford
Rachel A. Pollard
Sarah Lutz
Tracie Contois
Heather Harjer
Hana Polom
Hassan Chouaib
Randee Dunigan

1 Sakera.   2 Penny Mack and Davett.   3 Dino, my security.
4 Cousins Tierra and Mande.   5 Face and Darryl.   6 Joi Prego.
7 Big Bro Toni.   8 Aunt Ressie.   9 Julie with Fasheed and Fashaad.
10 Dallas dancing to "Creep."   11 Tony Rich at my '95 housewarming.
12 Nechole and Cousin Donnie.

1 Xscape, me, Jamie Brown, Sister 2 Sister, and Hiram Hicks.
2 Brat and me at a '97 party at Esso's.   3 Lil' Kim and me.   4 Dressed up
for an award show in Barbados in '97.   5 Shanti and me, Christmas '98.
6 TLC—'98 Fanmail shot.

1 *Vibe* photo shoot.   2 TLC in Japan.   3 Elton John and me.   4 RuPaul, Lisa, and me at the "No Scrubs" shoot.   5 Me and Dolly, friend and manager.   6 Photographer Daylen and me.   7 *Rolling Stone* photo shoot.

NATIONAL ACADEMY OF RECORDING ARTS & SCIENCES

TLC

BEST R&B ALBUM – 1995

"CRAZYSEXYCOOL"

i wanna be free

music is a way of life for me
maybe just "for outsiders
    it's hard to see"
how this business
can tear you apart
make you act evil
scar your heart

the best thing to do
is control it at your best
watch over your business
never let it rest

it's been said
over and over again
you control it
never let it win

i should sing because i'm happy
sing because i'm free
but somehow i feel like
this business has made
a slave of me

one day i will break my shackles,
run as far as i can
continue to make music
as long as you remain my fans

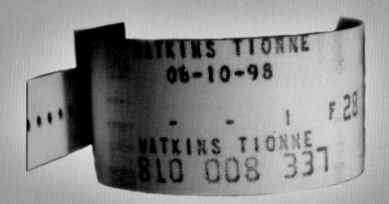

a sick life

when you're ill
your mood is strange
tryin' not to feel sorry for yourself
and tryin' to find someone to blame

you have to stay positive
that should be your only choice
being negative makes it worse
unhappiness shows
in the tone of your voice

things happen for a reason
just as we're born to survive
have hope and believe
that should help you stay alive

lie (lī) *n.* [as lyge] **1.** A false hood; untrut **2.** Anything that deceives. **3.** A charge that one has lied.

what's my name

i fly out your mouth
and deep from your soul
i'm your closest friend
so i am told

i get you through problems
truly and with speed
when you can't think of anything else,
i'm the first you need

i have hurt many
but that's not my fault
you own my body
therefore i am caught

i don't like you
but yet you love me
you've lost all you had
and you still can't see

what makes you use me
just tell all, the truth
guess it was something
you missed as a youth

hi! my name is "lie"
please leave me alone
but people will always use me

let the truth be known

why

why is a question
most times never known
life would be too easy
if the answers easily shown

who knows why
the sky is blue
who knows why
god made you you

things happen for a reason
the reason may be a test
everyone's destiny is chosen
before they're laid to rest

wishes

if you had one wish
what would you choose
i'm sure something special
or to walk in one's shoes

it's so deep
when a person has to say
they want to meet a star
and have it that way

if you're a celeb
who has met a wish foundation child
that was their one and only wish
take it to heart
don't take it mild

give your time
that's the least you could do
and remember their last wish
in the world was to meet you

murder

it's

everything grows in stages
just like one, two, and three
what would have happened
if my mother got rid of me

an infant turns to toddler
toddler turns to child
child to a teenager
to being an adult
isn't that wild

how can you say
an embryo and fetus are nothing
you're just making an excuse
because you know you're killing something!

FOR SALE

i met someone today
and guess what he said
do ya wanna come with me
can i please take you to bed

i said no mista
what be yo name
a name that's unforgettable
and never known to be lame

he says are you a runaway
i said mmm maybe so
he said i'll take care of you
why don't you be my ho

i said what does ho mean
is that something bad
he said no my dear
if not you'll wish you had

why is that sir
he says i can make you rich
give you everything you
    hope for
but don't tell anybody
    don't be a snitch

if it's not wrong
why can't i tell
i don't like people in my
    business
and if they ask tell 'em to
    go to hell

trick for me make money
but only at your will
how could you turn
    this down
makin' that dollar bill

i guess i'll pass
go back home where i
    should be
being out on the streets
made me learn the streets
    are not for me

violence can be the way for some

sometimes it seems better

to fight than to run

cornered into gangs

given little choice or none

if you don't have to join, don't

the amounts who have

equal a great sum

not a punk.

i understand sometimes

there is no way out

but if there is, take advantage

and get the hell out

NOTICE OF INTENTION TO DISPOSE OF MOTOR VEHI
(California Civil Code Section 2983.2)

Date of Mailin

YOU MAY NOT REINSTATE

THE MOTOR VEHICLE HAS BEEN CONCEALED OR REMOVED FROM T

AVOID REPOSSESSION.

YOUR ACCOUNT IS SERIOUSLY PAST DUE. PLEASE

FINAL NOTICE

O AVOID CUTOFF, THE

BILL MUST BE PAID B

THIS IS THE ONLY NO

ICE YOU WILL RECEIV

priorities

the word can be confusing
let's define what it means
what's important, first
close, far, now or in between

do we take things for granted
and put the not-so-important things first
do what's better last
and the worst things first

gamble with rent money
go party instead of work
put things off until later
so on and so forth

have you done these things
and your problems still exist
maybe you should learn responsibility
and make that the *first* priority on your list!

late night calls

this belongs to me
this between my legs
if i say no
find no reason to beg

don't force yourself
upon me, that is called rape
treat me like an animal
and feel up my shape

but where i went wrong
when you asked
i came along

late night calls
are for one thing
in the middle of the night
it's a booty call or a fling

i should have known better
who's to blame
myself or him
knowing he wants one thing

to sum up what's said
if a man tries
to take you to bed
don't go just to say no
just stay home instead

"Girl, you better get with him, so he's ugly, but he got money."

"What kind of car do you drive?"

"He didn't even speak, but at least I got to sleep with him."

"Can I go home with you?"

"Where you stay at?"

"So you play ball?...Professionally?"

"Can I come backstage?"

"What hotel are you at?"

"I'm gonna have his baby... that's a paycheck for life."

"Will you take me shopping?"

"Girl, this dress is gonna get him."

"If I do him once, he's hooked."

the groupie

being whores come at their best
they wiggle their butts
or flash their breasts

give her insides to a
man she doesn't know
who drools all over her
and treats her like a ho

is it love lost in family
or no self respect
her mother's traits
or just disrespect

what makes a woman
chase a man for fame and cheese
to get what she can
material or a name
bitch, please!

you're simple never
forget this
and you're cheap at best
to sleep with fame and fortune
what's the rest?

you spoke the words
"i slept with a star"
but nine times out of ten
they don't care who you are

being a groupie is a
hell of a life
some are even
made to be wives

some are smart hoes
and some are dumb
if you're getting screwed
for nothing did he at least cum

if you feel good about yourself
being married to a sum
your heart must be shallow
and very numb

the woman's body was
really made for one
if you have children
i feel for your daughter or son

sluts be careful
and you know who you are
being promiscuous hides
an invisible scar

i'm so blessed to have you in my life
i hope i've been a good enough daughter
without bringing too much stress in your life!
i love you in so many ways
you're more than just my mom

you're a person who's
touched me
helped me
kept me strong
even if that minute
you couldn't be there
your voice stayed strong
and remained in my head

you gave me life
and taught me how to live
now it's my turn
is there something i can give

thank you for being
and for being my friend
i will always have your back
the way you've had mine
through thick and thin
in the hospital
you were always there
seeing your face
gave me strength
to get out of there

you're a major part of me
in my heart everyday you live
and to you gayle watkins
this poem i give
to my mother
i love you!

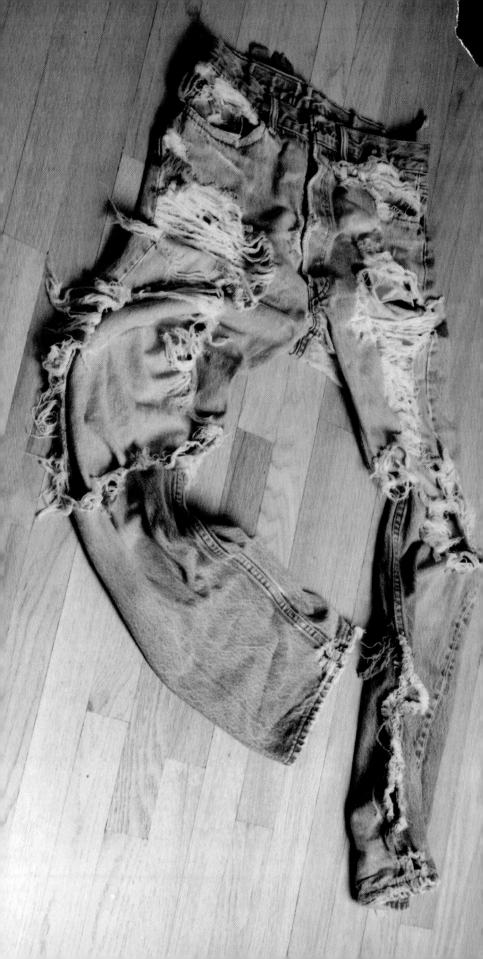

OXTAILS

Ingredients:
2 pkgs. beef oxtails
1 onion (sliced)
    Lawrey's Seasoning Salt
    garlic salt
    black pepper
1/4 cup flour

Directions:
1. Boil oxtails in a big pot with water filled 2 inches over the meat.
2. Place sliced onions in the pot with the meat.
3. Season with Lawrey's, garlic salt, and black pepper.
4. Boil on medium heat for 6–8 hours (depending on how tender the oxtails become).
5. Season once every hour.
6. During the last hour, mix flour with 1/2 cup water. Stir until all lumps have dissolved.
7. Pour flour mixture over oxtails. Increase heat and boil for 30 minutes.
8. Reduce heat and let simmer.
9. Eat on!

my favorite things...

TACO CASSEROLE

Ingredients:
1 tomato (diced)
1 onion (diced)
1 green pepper (diced)
1 large bag Doritos
1 pkg. taco mix seasoning
1 lb. ground beef or turkey ground
4 pkgs. muenster cheese (shredded)
1 head of iceberg lettuce

Directions:
1. **Brown ground beef (or turkey ground) in a skillet.**
2. Add taco seasoning mix.
3. Preheat oven to 375°F.
4. **Crumble Doritos on the bottom of a 9" x 13" baking dish.**
5. Add meat mixture.
6. Layer green peppers, tomatoes, onions, and lettuce.
7. Add shredded cheese on top.
8. Bake in oven for 25–30 minutes or until brown.

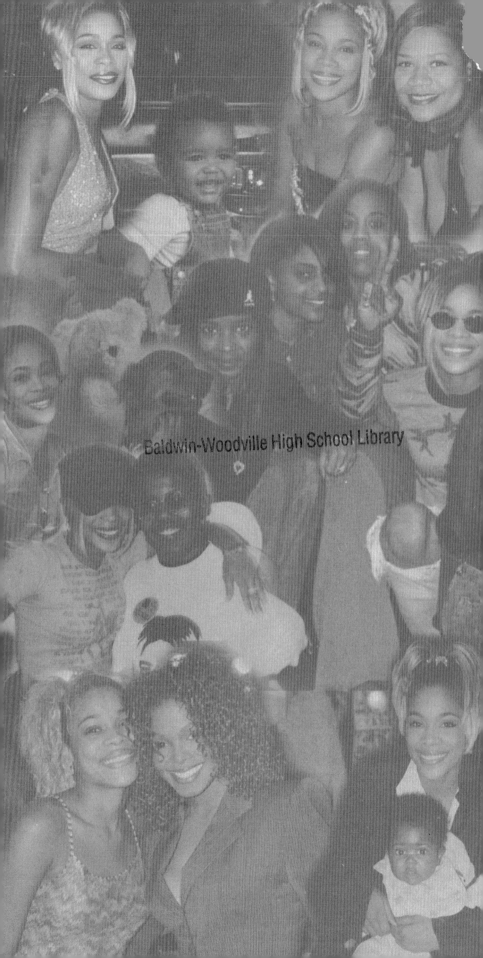